Dear Safi –

   Congratulations on your graduation!
What a star you are!
                         Love,
                            The Christman
                               Family

ACCUMULATED INSIGHT

A COLLECTION OF LIFE LESSONS

H. STUART VALENTINE IV

Accumulated Insight

A Collection of Life Lessons

© 2017 H. Stuart Valentine IV

Print ISBN: 978-1-54390-951-7

eBook ISBN: 978-1-54390-952-4

TABLE OF CONTENTS

This book is dedicated to my two children who were the inspiration for its writing. It is my hope that in some small way the thoughts inside can serve as a resource as they navigate through life.

There are certain times that you stop and assess where you are in life. I recently went through one such moment. Within a two-week period, I turned fifty years old and also dropped my son off for his first year at boarding school. The combination of these two events caused me to reflect on where I had been, where I was going, and just how fast time was flying by. As we prepared my son to go off to school and be on his own for the first time, I gave some thought to the best advice with which I could provide him. I wished that I had compiled all my "words of wisdom" to present to him for guidance. I also had gone to boarding school when I was sixteen and, looking back, it would have been very helpful if I had been given a similar resource to which I could have referred.

Then it occurred to me that I was actually in a position to make this happen for my son. It takes us most of our lives to accumulate lessons learned through the successes and failures we endure. By the time we figure out how life works, there is not a lot of time left to put this accumulated wisdom into action and we tend to think that the rest of the world should figure these things out on its own. As a matter of fact, many feel it is a rite of passage. They might say, "Well, I didn't have anyone sit me down and tell me how the world works, so let the youngsters figure it out on their own." I am not one of those people. I feel that if I have figured a few things out during my half a century on this earth, it is my duty to share this information with my children and anyone else that might find it useful. As a parent, my job is to prepare my children as best as possible for dealing with life and all that it might throw at them. So

I decided I would sit down and compile some of the life lessons that I have learned to this point so I could share them with my children and anyone else that would listen. It took me four years to achieve this, which leads me to another life lesson that is not included in this edition: Everything worth doing always takes a lot longer than you think it will. (Consider this lesson on the house.)

I have always felt that I am in a unique position in terms of the role models that I have been lucky enough to have in my life. I am still blessed, to this day, to have four different parental figures, which is amazing considering I am over the age of fifty. Both of my parents remarried after their divorce, and I have a very good relationship with both my parents and step-parents. Furthermore, three of my four grandparents lived into their nineties. For a man to have a father, stepfather, and grandfather all play a major role in his life is very unique. They all are very good people in completely different ways. Having all of these varied role models in my life has been invaluable as it has let me witness different philosophies and strategies on how to approach life. Most people are not afforded this luxury. Growing up, they see only one approach to life and, as a result, adopt this same approach when they get older. I, on the other hand, have been able to mold myself through the sound advice and example of many different influential people.

In compiling these words of wisdom for my son and daughter, it became apparent that there might be a use for them beyond my own children, for I am sure that many of these life lessons would show up on almost everyone's list if they were to also sit down and write them out. The life lessons that I present in this book could be useful to people of all ages, not just the young. A search engine is not exactly earth-shattering technology. All it does is cull through the Internet and present what it feels are the most useful items in regards to what you are searching for. This book is kind of the same thing. Nothing in it is exactly groundbreaking material. Some of the items in this book you may have figured out on your own at this point, some you may disagree with, and others may just be useful reminders while you go through certain situations in your life. I wrote this book with the most important audience in mind—my children. Anyone else that finds it helpful in some small way, while certainly very satisfying, is gravy.

Finally, there is one thing I want to make very clear before you move on to the first page. Listing these life lessons in no way indicates that I, myself, have mastered them. As mentioned later on, failure is perhaps the best educator. Some of these suggestions have been put forth because I have realized firsthand the benefits of excelling at them. However, I recognize the importance of others only because I continue to experience the downside of not being very good at them. I take solace in the fact that good coaches were often only average players.

CHAPTER 1

FAILURE IS A NECESSARY INGREDIENT TO SUCCESS

When I was in grade school, I was a decent student but certainly nothing extraordinary. I went off to prep school in Connecticut as a sophomore. In my first year at prep school, I had a less than stellar moment that ended up changing my future. One day, I showed up for history class and the teacher told us to put our books away (never something you want to hear). Sure enough, he passed out a surprise quiz. No big deal normally, but in this case I had not read the chapter assigned for homework. I got a zero on the quiz. I had to fight my way back from this for the rest of the semester. Short term, this was a devastating blow. Long term, it was a blessing, as shame is an intense motivator. I never wanted to experience that feeling again, and I vowed that I would never be unprepared for a class going forward. I never was. I went on to do well for the rest of the year in all of my classes. In my junior year, I turned it up several notches and ended up in the top ten in my class. Senior year, I was accepted to Yale University and won the Latin Prize at graduation.

Sometimes you have to take a step back to take two steps forward. This is because, for the right person, failure or disrespect can be the impetus to the long-term focus and determination needed to succeed. It is important to understand that very few leaders have had an uninterrupted rise to the top.

Just ask Tom Brady. As a Jets fan, it pains me to use him as an example, but he is the poster child for letting disappointment light a fire that would lead to greatness. Tom was selected with the 199th overall pick in the 2000 NFL draft. A quarterback out of Michigan who was totally overlooked as someone with potential. He started out as the fourth-string quarterback his first season. He is now considered one of the greatest quarterbacks of all time. Tom used the pain of being overlooked in the draft as motivation to become the best. He did this through intense preparation, which has never subsided. The entertainment field is full of similar success stories in which athletes, musicians, and actors were told they would never amount to anything only to go on to prove all their doubters wrong.

Conversely, the landscape is littered with examples of "sure things" that were never tested and ended up falling flat on their faces. Staying with the quarterback example, we need look no further than Todd Marinovich. Todd was one of the most highly touted athletes of the 1990s. From birth, his dad raised him to be an NFL quarterback. He monitored every single aspect of Todd's life. Todd sailed through high school as a famed QB and then went to USC to become their starting QB. However, once he got to college and had a little room to breathe, he started to unravel. He started to smoke marijuana at school. He was drafted in the first round and played for the Los Angeles Raiders. After playing some average games at QB, he eventually lost his starting job, started having major drug issues, and after being kicked out of the league, never played again in the NFL. He has spent much of his adult life getting into trouble with the law.

Pain is just as effective as a motivator. Many of the great musicians have gone through extremely difficult childhoods. However, they use their early strife to motivate them to make a better life for themselves and this pain comes through in their music.

Early failure builds the grit and fortitude it takes to succeed long term, but only if you allow it. Certainly we don't look to fail, but when it happens, it all comes down to how we respond. Winners learn and become energized by losing. They learn from the experience and use this knowledge to avoid repeating their actions. Losers stay down, don't get up, and tend to repeat their behavior, hoping for a different result.

CHAPTER 2

UNDERSTAND THE PAST, BUT DON'T FOCUS ON IT

I t is imperative that we all be students of history. By history I mean not only the world history we study in school, but also the recent history of our own lives. We often don't realize it, but we utilize our understanding of both of these types of history to make important decisions in our own lives all the time. In the big picture, we can predict the outcomes of national events as well as local ones based on what has happened in the past. We can use our understanding of how world leaders have fared over time to predict the outcome of current policies and behavior. The most renowned military generals have used their understanding of past battles to help them design current maneuvers. Economists and market strategists must rely on their knowledge of historical financial events to successfully predict future ones. As a leader in any field, it is imperative to have an understanding of the history of your group or organization in able to successfully lead it going forward.

On a micro level, we need to also apply the same logic to our own everyday lives. In order to fully understand ourselves, who we are, and how we will react to a given event, we must know our own personal history. This starts with understanding our parents and grandparents. Researching our lineage makes it easier to understand our own behavior and tendencies. It is helpful to know where our parents came from and what they have been through in order to achieve self-improvement. For instance, my aunt died of colon cancer at too young an age. After this event, my cousin contacted me and told me he had done some research and it turns out that our family seems to have a history of this disease. This is very useful information and affected my thought process going forward. Our family was not previously aware of this, therefore, his knowledge of the past might save others in the future. I immediately had a colonoscopy done at the age of thirty-five and have had them regularly since. The better your understanding of your own personal history, the better prepared you are to handle the future.

But be clear, while you want to understand history, you don't want to live in it. Focusing on the past is not a good thing. People who focus on the past are either egomaniacs stuck on some past achievement or status which they let define who they are or they are very bitter people who are disgruntled about some instance in which they feel they have been wronged. Either way, they are caught looking backwards, and it is not possible to look ahead if you are looking in the rearview mirror. As we will discuss next chapter, happy and successful people are always looking forward to tomorrow. If you are constantly talking about yesterday, you have given up on the fact that something better may be attainable in the future. This results in a loss of energy, drive, and meaningfulness. Focusing on today and tomorrow leads to a much healthier mental and physical state of being. You will find that the great leaders and influential people of our day don't like to talk about the past. They find this to be a complete waste of time and a drain of energy that could be better used to focus on today or, more importantly, tomorrow.

CHAPTER 3

ANNIE HAD IT RIGHT

The Broadway musical "Annie" has a signature song entitled "Tomorrow" where the little orphan girl sings, "Tomorrow, tomorrow, I love you tomorrow, you're only a day away." In order to maintain a positive attitude while surrounded by despair, she sings of always focusing on what the future might bring. This little girl learns at a young age the key to making good things happen—a laser focus on the future. All great leaders have this personality trait. In order to shape the future, you must be able to envision it. Great people always seem to be able to see two moves ahead, just like world-renowned chess players. You will find that an unwavering focus on the future is a common characteristic of all influential people.

As I was taking my driving lessons when I was just sixteen, the instructor kept emphasizing not to focus your eyes just over the hood of the car but, rather, well down the road. This allows you to see potential issues and have time to react to them. Life is no different. Just take a look at the interviews with wrongly incarcerated inmates being released from prison after decades of serving time for crimes they did not commit. I am always stunned by these stories. These people come out and seem to be at peace, not bitter, and very focused on what they are going to do going forward. How is this possible? The answer lies in the fact that these people have figured out that in order to survive and stay mentally healthy, all they have is their belief that the future will be better than today. Focusing on the past will not do them any good. Meanwhile, you and I tend to get irritated when we are forced to stand in line for more than two minutes for a four-dollar coffee. We can learn a lot from these people.

Another good example is Thomas Edison. Thomas Edison was most likely the greatest American inventor in history with over 1000 patents to his name. His first breakthrough invention was the phonograph, which for the first time, allowed us to record someone's voice. This paved the way for the record player and many other inventions that changed our lives. At the time, this invention made him world-renowned. But he kept on going. He then discovered the invention that would change all of our lives—the electric light bulb. This made Edison the biggest name of his day. He was overwhelmed with notoriety. However, this quickly annoyed him because it kept him from being able to move forward and come up with the next great invention. He could have stopped there and basked in the glory of the greatest invention of the century, but he did not want to focus on the past. He eventually moved his team to a secluded dwelling where he could not be bothered so he could keep his focus on tomorrow and not yesterday. One night his laboratory went up in flames. As he watched the flames devour his beloved state of the art laboratory, he was making a list of all the things he would need to do the next day to get back on his feet. Even before the fire was out, he had moved on to the future. Edison went on to obtain patents that led to major innovations in motion pictures and telecommunications. If Edison had stopped after the phonograph and turned his focus to the past, we might be still sitting in the dark.

CHAPTER 4

A CLEARING SHOWER

The most important thing I have learned during my short time on earth is that one's outlook on life is the single greatest factor in determining how life will turn out for you. Now don't get me wrong, I will take a little luck and a lot of skill when I can get it, but if you look at all of the great leaders and "successful" people that surround you, it will become obvious that they all have one thing in common—a very positive attitude.

The good news is that this is a trait that is easily learned. I, myself, wasted a lot of time early in life not understanding this simple fact. Not that I had a bad attitude; I never did. However, I never had a very positive outlook. I grew up with a fairly pessimistic view of the world. Expect the worst and you will never be disappointed. It took quite a while for me to figure out that this attitude is like running a road race with three-pound weights on your ankles. For one thing, negative thoughts drain you of all your energy. More importantly, no one wants to be around negative people. The easiest way to become positive if it does not come easily is to surround yourself with people who are positive. When you see others go through life with this important characteristic and see the results it brings them, it will eventually rub off on you. Remember, you control whom you surround yourself with. If you believe that your current pool of friends or colleagues does not have this perspective, then make a change. Always focus on the future, not the past. The past has no bearing on what will happen in the future. So don't waste a lot of time thinking about how great or bad things were yesterday because it won't affect what may happen to you today. I am not saying that you shouldn't have some sense of realism and be cognizant of your limits or boundaries, but it is important to have positive goals and a sense that any task can be accomplished.

The world is full of very bright and skilled people. However, the business people, athletes, and artists who rise to the top are usually the ones with the most positive perspective. Tiger Woods is a perfect example of the role a positive mental state can play. For a decade, he dominated the sport of golf as no one else had before him. When any other player would get close to taking a title from him, Tiger's intensely effusive confidence would cause his opponents to wilt. He rolled off a string of major tournament wins. However, after the well-publicized trouble in his personal life, it certainly seems that a very slight change in his mental composition occurred and he has not won a Major since then. While he certainly has had some physical issues to attend to, it seems that his powerfully confident attitude was affected by the troubles off the course.

Positivity and confidence give us the edge that pushes us from good to great. The best role model I have for this is my stepfather. The sun is always shining in his world. Several years ago, he had a major stroke on the evening of his 89th birthday. When he awoke in the hospital, he could not talk, swallow, or move anything on his left side. Now this is a person who has had a highly successful life on anyone's scale of achievement and is the most positive person I have ever known. When he took the family to Hawaii to celebrate his 65th birthday, he made a tee time for us to play a famous course there. The morning we woke up to play, it was pouring rain. We looked at him, expecting to see a disappointed man. However, he simply turned to us at breakfast and said, "It is a clearing shower. We will be fine."

Twenty-four years later, when we first saw him lying in the hospital bed in this difficult state after his stroke, it would have been easy to understand if he felt like he didn't have the energy to come back from this devastating blow. It was his mental state we worried about most. However, these concerns went out the window when I saw him for the first time after his stroke, lying in his hospital bed. Since he could not talk, he grabbed the chalkboard and wrote me a message. It said, "I heard the Super Bowl is coming here in two years. Make sure you get us some tickets." After that, I told my mother he was going to be fine. He was back on his feet in six months.

CHAPTER 5

TRUST YOUR GUT... IT KNOWS

Some people can sit in a meeting and have no sense of their surroundings. Other people have a keen understanding of not only who is in the room, but the energy they are emitting. I am one of those people. I notice what others are doing, whether they are paying attention, if they are mad, happy, bored, etc. At times, people are so focused on what they are doing that they have no awareness of what is going on around them. This sense of your surroundings can be very helpful at times. When you are paying close attention to anything for a period of time, you are more likely to get a gut feeling about anything that may happen. I am also this way about my health, stock prices, game trends, and many other things. I get a lot of "gut" feelings. The downside to this awareness is that it can cause one to be frequently distracted which can result in the undertaking of frivolous activities. However, I have learned it is always good to go with your gut feelings when you have them. Mainly because they are often correct, but also, if you don't, and things don't work out, it is much harder to get over it if you ignored your instincts.

I attended a boarding school in Connecticut for my high school years. I eventually became a very good student. During my

Junior year, I went to my cubby one day to get my books. Back then, each student had an open cubby area where you kept all your books and notebooks during the school day. One day, I noticed my history notebook was missing on the eve of a big history test. I knew exactly where my notebook had been and realized immediately that it had been taken. I had a "gut" feeling that a female student in my class had taken the notebook. However, since at boarding schools boys were not allowed in the girls' dorms, I had to figure out how I was going to investigate this possibility. Keep in mind, I had no meaningful information as to where this notebook was, I was working simply off of my gut. I decided to ask the roommate of this girl if she would check their dorm room. This was a very risky thing for me because if I was wrong I would look like an idiot, but I went ahead and asker her. The girl could not understand why I thought it might be her roommate, but said she would take a look in their room. She came to me at dinnertime and told me that she didn't find anything. Now, this is where most people would say okay and back off, but like a good poker player, I raised the ante, pushed all my chips into the middle of the table, and insisted that she go back to the room and do a more thorough check. She thought I was absolutely crazy. I just had a sense that she was not telling me the truth when she told me she had checked the room. I asked that she go back to the room and check again, and she reluctantly agreed. Approximately one hour later, I got a knock on my door from a hall mate who told me there was someone outside that wanted to see me. It was the same girl I had spoken to about my suspicions. Her eyes were as big as half dollars and she held in her hand my history notebook. In total disbelief, all she said was, "How did you know that my roommate had taken your notebook?" I told her I didn't, I just had a gut feeling. Now, keep in mind, this was a serious offense on the part of the girl that took the notebook. Stealing someone else's notes could easily get her expelled from the school. She must have been terrified. However, the next day when it was time to go to class to take the test, I waited for everyone to take a seat and then simply sat down right next to her and quietly put my notebook where she could see it. I never mentioned it to anyone. True story. The gut knows.

CHAPTER 6

COMMUNICATING IS KEY

One of the key skills needed to succeed in all aspects of life is the ability to communicate. It is a common skill found in all great leaders. To lead a group of people effectively, you need a clear goal, but more importantly, you need to be able to communicate the benefits of achieving this goal and how you intend to accomplish it. Communicating does not need to be an elaborate or complicated process. In fact, it is much more effective for one to communicate in a clear, concise, and passionate way. To effectively persuade people, you have to be able to clearly lay out your vision. Having a good cause is not enough unless it is presented in a decisive manner.

A former CEO once told me that he wasn't totally sure how a certain area of his company operated. Very confused, I asked him how he could not know all the details of that department if he was the head of the entire firm. He said, "I am a communicator. I put good people in place to run these departments that are experts in their fields. My job is to communicate where we are going as an entire entity." Back in his day, he would address the entire firm at the end of every week on a "squawk box" which was a small, speaker-like box on the desk of all employees across the country. I had the opportunity to sit in on one of his addresses, which was very simple in nature. He would congratulate the firm on certain achievements and update everyone on where they were in the progress of overall company goals. You could not help but feel energized after one of his talks with a clear sense of where you were going as a group.

The lack of this type of communication is a large part of the problem with American business today. I do not think most employees have a sense of the overall goals of their company or even their own department for that matter. The companies that communicate well seem to thrive, but these seem to be the exceptions rather than the rule. I believe communicating, in all its forms, is a lost art. People have become afraid to communicate face-to-face or even over the phone. Society has become too comfortable hiding behind their voicemail and e-mail. The good news is that, as a result, it is very easy to stand out. Spend more time communicating in an effective manner and you will quickly separate yourself from others. Use it to your advantage. Many firms have gone through so many mergers and acquisitions that they have become conglomerations of different employees who often end up receiving very little direction. Today, so much value is placed on finding CEOs with strategic skills that allow them to determine with whom to merge, who to acquire, and what to divest. Communicating a vision is not at the top of the list for these people, so I am hard pressed to call them leaders. The result is leaders of companies who are more focused on motivating stock prices as opposed to people, and this has resulted in employees who lack a sense of empowerment or loyalty.

The general exception to this trend seems to be the technology industry. The leaders of these companies are passionate and, most importantly, seem to regularly communicate with their employees about their goals of changing the way the world works and how they are going to achieve this. You will find that the most successful leaders in the military, politics, education, and sports possess these same principles and skills as well.

The timing and frequency of your communication is also a key factor. Take a good coach for instance. If you were to give a rousing speech every single game or each time things were going wrong, your players would eventually tune it out, and your communication would lose its effectiveness. A good coach knows when to press the button. A good communicator must also know when the best thing to say is nothing at all.

Finally, good communication is also very important outside the office. Certainly, communication of simple goals and expectations is vital between spouses and with the rest of the family as well. The family unit is a team that needs to work together just like any unified group at the office or on the field. Everyone wants to be part of team, have a role in the overall game plan, and have a sense of where they are going. Ever sit down with your spouse, parents, or children and ask them what their near and long-term goals are? What they would change if they could? You might be surprised by the answers. Many spouses go through their days trying to achieve goals they have shared with no one. They assume their spouses are okay with these goals or even know what they are. No matter what the setting, the more often you stop to communicate with those around you, even if just briefly, the more likely you are to avoid a really serious conversation one day that will alter the course of your life.

CHAPTER 7

KNOW YOUR AUDIENCE

This applies whether you are speaking to one person or one hundred. I once received a phone call from my manager at work. While he was my manager, we were also friends. In the middle of a friendly conversation, he began to casually ask me my opinion on our district boss. I made the huge mistake of giving it to him. While not overly negative, I gave my honest feedback. It turns out this was not a good idea. I figured out later that he was testing me on behalf of our boss to see if I was "on the team." Our district boss at the time was intensely cliquey. He had a group of guys who made up his posse. My manager was a key member of this group and, looking back on it, this phone call was clearly a test to see if I could be trusted to become part of this inner circle.

As you can imagine, I failed miserably. I did not see myself as part of this group of people and, unconsciously, giving my honest opinion was probably my way of distancing myself from them. As a result, I was never brought in to this inner circle, and it definitely impacted this part of my career. Always be cognizant of who you are addressing. Know who they are, how they operate, their motives, and with whom they are friends. This should determine what you say to whom.

Once on a visit to a branch of the firm, I was brought in to someone's office. This person, knowing that I worked in the corporate headquarters, wanted to make sure I knew he had grievances. He proceeded to say, "You want to see what is wrong with this company?" and held up a marketing kit that had been made available to him by corporate. He went on and on about how it was useless and a prime example of how the firm was misguided in its focus.

What he didn't know was that he was speaking to the husband of the person who had spent the last year of her life creating this piece and working on this project. I never let this person know how he had embarrassed himself, but let's just say that my relationship with him was never the same after his tirade. You just never know whom you are talking to sometimes and so it always pays to think before you speak.

Another thing to consider and something that has consistently created issues for me is to be careful with your sense of humor. I have a very dry sense of humor that gets me in trouble all of the time. My frequent use of sarcasm is a lot of fun for me because I can make fun of someone without the person even knowing it. My good friends are aware of and appreciate this sense of humor. However, when it comes out with those that I don't know as well, I often get myself in trouble. The line between sarcasm and being straightforward can get very blurry, and as a result I sometimes end up hurting people's feelings.

A former Chairman and CEO told me he kept a copy of every speech he ever gave and that he wrote all of his own speeches, which is unheard of these days. He filed all of his speeches away for future reference and made notes of exactly who would be in the audience. He didn't obviously list every person that was there, but made notes of who the group was and some of the key people in attendance. He would not write a speech without knowing specifically whom he would be addressing. He cross-referenced these files whenever he wrote a new speech so as never to be redundant. Now, I am not suggesting that we adopt these same detailed measures, as most of us are not CEOs. However, other top executives could take some tips today from his meticulous methods, and we can certainly learn a lesson about the importance of knowing your audience no matter what the situation.

CHAPTER 8

LIVE YOUR WHOLE LIFE LIKE OTHERS DO IN THE FINAL YEARS OF THEIRS

Ever notice that as people get older, they tend to let go of their anger towards others and trend toward peace as opposed to conflict? Sure, the elderly get cranky about intensely little things like the cost of gas and any change to the broadcasting schedule of "Wheel of Fortune." However, in terms of relationships, they tend to try to mend old fences and become more welcoming to those they used to ignore. This is because, as they lose their sources of influence and other things that used to garner them a sense of importance, they can't afford to be picky as to who might show them attention and make them feel important. Furthermore, anger requires a lot more energy than contentment and, as we get older, we begin to come to peace with ourselves.

It is generally the middle-aged that hold grudges and let anger build up. They are prone to letting temporary factors influence how they approach life. These temporary factors almost always have something to do with letting the behavior of others affect us in a disproportionate way. We may tend to get overly bothered by someone at work who is moving ahead faster or getting away with things, or upset with an ex-spouse after a divorce. We can let petty things bother us, like the lifestyle of our friends that maybe we can't afford. In other words, we let the behavior of others negatively impact the way we view the world. What is even more maddening is that these people are, in many cases, not intentionally trying to hurt us, but we are letting their actions get to us.

These issues have little impact on the elderly or the young in terms of happiness. I currently have two parents and one step-parent who are all over 75 years old along with one step-parent who is in his nineties. I was also lucky enough to have three out of four grandparents live to their nineties. I noticed a trend that as they approached their elderly years, they seemed to be relatively immune to all the people that used to drive them crazy. They started to "let bygones be bygones" and, more often than not, considered everything "water under the bridge."

So, I asked myself, "If I am going to let this anger go eventually, why not just let it go now as much as possible? Why hang on to it for another twenty or thirty years for no reason? My advice to you is, take a look at the sources of your current anger and anxiety and release as many of them as possible now which will allow you to live a more peaceful life for a much longer period of time.

CHAPTER 9

"KEEPING UP WITH THE JONESES" HAS AN ADVERSE EFFECT ON THE QUALITY OF YOUR LIFE

I f you stop and take inventory of all of the decisions you make that are at least partially based on what others will think or how you want to be perceived by others, I think you will be surprised by the outcome. Of course, it is sometimes difficult to be honest in this regard. I am sure, for example, there are plenty of young parents that feel that the Mercedes S series in which they drive their kids to school in was purchased as a result of a thorough review of options and subsequent conclusion that this particular car best suited their needs, budget, and driving requirements. You never know when you are going to have to go from zero to sixty in ten seconds in that difficult-to-maneuver school pick-up line. There was one guy who used to work with me in the same office and he would always show up to work in a different high-end sports car. For a while it was a Porsche, then a Maserati, Ferrari, and so on. So we all thought, "Wow, that guy is really doing well." It turns out, he was just a member of a car club and, for a membership fee, could take home different cars every few months. I am not saying that he didn't do well and make a lot of money, but it just seems like this is going well out of your way to make an impression on others.

For those that can be honest with themselves, we make many decisions every week based on our notion of how we will be perceived by others. This process of "keeping up with the Joneses" causes serious anxiety and drains our energy, never mind the impact on our household budget. The phrase "keeping up with" in itself suggests that you are not the pacesetter in this race and that you are naturally chasing from behind. This is stressful in and of itself. But when you factor in the strong possibility that the "Joneses" themselves are probably highly leveraged, you begin to feel stupid about your relentless pursuit. I am not saying that you shouldn't pursue the things in life that make you happy, whatever they are, but what I am suggesting is that you make these decisions without any concern for the approval of others. Find a way of life that is comfortable for you and you will end up surrounding yourself with the right people. Being honest and true to yourself is always attractive and requires less energy than the alternative. The energy you save can then be put to use in a more constructive manner that will allow you to live a more fulfilling and successful life.

CHAPTER 10

FOCUS ON THE LITTLE THINGS TO SEPARATE YOURSELF

These days most people focus on trying to hit the proverbial "grand slam" in everything they do in an effort to separate themselves from others whether at home or in the office. This driving need to make the highlight reel has gotten out of control and has had its effects on our society. People are very busy building a brand for themselves. One just has to look at people's social media pages as an example. The world seems bent on garnering respect through a series of pictures and posts instead of actual accomplishments. This path to notoriety is a more difficult one. After all, it is much easier to accumulate base hits than grand slams, and they occur much more frequently.

Few people understand that, in today's world, simply focusing on the little things every day will eventually separate you from most others. Sounds so basic, but these days very few people are doing it.

In business, very simple things like answering your phone, responding to emails, being flexible, coming through for your clients at the price and time you promised has become the exception not the rule. How you greet people, approach tasks, follow up on things, and communicate are all very noticeable to others and make an immediate impression. Outside of the office, be positive, look people in the eye, and take an interest in what people are saying and doing. Be honest, follow through on what you say, treat people nicely, and it will go a long way to getting you to the top of whatever mountain you are trying to climb. It is sad that these days these extremely simple things separate you from so many others. My daughter's school recently named a new headmaster. In the beginning of the school year, it was clear he was trying to make a good impression. As we dropped the kids off at school, he sat outside the front door and shook the hands of the students as they entered the school. I thought this was a nice touch to start his tenure, but it eventually became apparent that this was not a short-term ploy to make an impression because, as the cold days of February came around, he was still out there every single morning, shaking kids' hands. Two years later, he is still doing it every day. With this very simple act, he was sending the following signals to the school community: First, that he cared about every student that came through the door. Second, that there was no job within the school that he was not willing to do. Finally, he was making it clear that he was accessible to all. This one simple act said so much. So, to continue with the baseball analogies, stop trying to be the Reggie Jackson of your community and focus on being the Derek Jeter. Be known for how you play the game all season long as opposed to just being Mr. October.

CHAPTER 11

IN ORDER TO HAVE GOOD FRIENDS YOU HAVE TO WORK AT IT

As you know, in order to be very good at something you have to dedicate yourself to it and make it a priority. However, most people don't think that this applies to anything other than their careers and hobbies. If it is important to you to have good friends as well, it is a mistake to overlook the need to apply hard work to this area of your life. First of all, you must understand that there is a big difference between acquaintances, friends, and good friends. The amount you have of the former two categories is really irrelevant, the number of the latter is not.

I, myself, require good friends with whom to share my life for I have figured out that happiness is about people and not things, titles, or achievements. No matter how social you are, you will eventually need good friends and the more you have the better. I can't tell you when you will need them, but at some point in your life, their importance will be immeasurable. Making, and more importantly maintaining, good friendships takes work. It takes time and effort to see and communicate with people regularly.

Furthermore, a good friend requires you to sacrifice your time and energy sometimes purely for the benefit of the other person. Most people ignore the fact that it requires commitment to establish and sustain good friendships. It takes no effort to secure an acquaintance and a relatively small amount to establish a friend. However, good friends are a totally different category, and the energy required rises exponentially. That is why the law of diminishing returns can come into play with good friends. Since it does take time, and sacrifices are required to keep them, it becomes difficult to keep a large number of good friends at once. Therefore, it is essential that you give serious thought as to who falls in this category.

I recommend assessing your friendships on a periodic basis just like you do other things in your life to make sure they are in line with your core values. It is important to keep in mind that your good friends can be a strong indicator of who you are as a person. As you have most likely heard before, you are a reflection of whom you surround yourself with. I have had several friendships that at some point I realized were out of balance. It occurred to me that I was doing all of the work in maintaining that relationship. I was always the one reaching out and making the effort. As a result, I decided to stop exerting the energy. Good friendships, like most other things in your life, rebalance themselves. Just remember that friendships that are important to you require just as much work on your part as theirs. So stop investing in friends that don't invest in you. I am a very social person. I like to host gatherings of various sizes. I recently turned fifty years old and had a large party. I used the invitation list as a chance to analyze my friendships. After review, I took a few people off the list because I just felt like what was once a mutual relationship had become lopsided. It is funny how life works because soon after the party, some of these people reached out to me suggesting that we get together. My sense is that they also came to a realization that friendships take work on both ends and should never be taken for granted.

CHAPTER 12

THE MORE YOU APPEAR TO WANT SOMETHING, THE LESS LIKELY YOU ARE TO ACQUIRE IT

This may be confusing to most because we have been taught that in order to achieve something we have to focus on it and dedicate ourselves to the task. This is true. However, they key word here is "appear." It is one thing to have a goal or something that you want to achieve. It is another to wear it on your sleeve so that it is outwardly apparent and becomes an obsession. Obsessions rarely end well, and desperation is highly unattractive. I will admit that there is a fine line here, but like most things in life, the key is not to cross it.

We have all heard the expression "a watched pot never boils." If I look back on job interviews that I really wanted to go well, I realize that I didn't get any of these positions. This is because anxiety and desperation become evident to others no matter how hard you try to conceal them and this eventually works against you. Similarly, we all have those people we really wanted to date who never seemed to have any interest in us or the client we wanted to land that we just couldn't. Chances are that overzealousness caused us to make our move too early or abruptly and this turned the person in a different direction. We all want to be courted, but not stalked. Our anxiety tends to come out when we over-focus on something. We tense up, our personality is altered, and in some cases our decision-making becomes compromised.

Sports often present us with examples of this phenomenon. When we really want to win a match or game, we tighten up and our peak performance becomes difficult to achieve. Do you think it's a coincidence that once Tiger Woods started focusing on winning majors to try and beat Jack Nicklaus's record he could no longer win at all. For the rest of us mortal golfers, if we are having a great round on the front nine, we often implode on the back nine and end up with a median score. This is because we tense up and have negative thoughts about blowing it. We tend to subconsciously revert to our comfort level. I have learned not to look at my scorecard after nine holes, and I try to focus on a conversation with someone that I am playing with to distract me. Look at what happened to Serena Williams when she came so close to achieving the calendar Grand Slam—a rare feat in tennis when one person wins all four major tournaments in the same calendar year. She won the first three and then was in the semifinals of the US Open playing a clearly inferior opponent. However, she tightened up in this match and ended up losing. She was one and a half matches away from completing this monumental task and fell short.

Wanting something so badly causes us to change our behavior and leads us to do things we would never do when relaxed. This is what separates true champions and great leaders. They seem to have an incredible ability to block out external distractions and control their emotions in very stressful situations. Their behavior and demeanor remains constant no matter what the situation, which allows them perform at their highest level when most needed.

Focusing on an outcome tends to preclude it. Therefore, when you really want something, try to make it part of some larger goal that you are trying to achieve.

CHAPTER 13

DON'T LET THE CHICKENS OUT IN THE FIRST PLACE
(because they always come home to roost)

C omplacency creates laziness. Laziness results in bad habits. Bad habits can ruin you. As we repeatedly continue down certain paths without immediate repercussions, we quickly lose sight of the risks. With costs dormant, we slowly move to the path of least resistance. This path feels good for a long while...until statistics eventually take over and we must pay for our laziness. Careless behavior always seems to rear its ugly head at the wrong time. Actually, it is just statistics playing out. It's not that we have to be thorough all the time; we don't. But we must understand that each time that we choose to cut corners or ignore risks, we are simply increasing the odds that something bad will eventually happen. Why do young people continue to smoke when they know it is highly destructive to their health? It is because they can't quantify the risks. It is difficult for twenty-one-year-olds to properly absorb the repercussion of their actions since they can't envision what their life will look like forty or fifty years down the road. Without an understanding of risks, immediate returns are easy to trade.

When I worked as a branch manager in the financial industry, a story went viral amongst the managers before there was such a thing as "viral." One day the CEO of the entire firm was out in our territory for a business meeting. He decided to make an unannounced visit to one of the branch offices in the area, a practice not uncommon for him. He walked into the office and asked to see the manager. The receptionist didn't seem to recognize the CEO. When she told the manager he had a guest, the manager told the receptionist he would be out in a bit. The CEO sat in the reception area of the office, and the manager kept him waiting and waiting and waiting. When you are a branch manager of a financial services firm, there are few times when an unexpected person asking to see the manager is a good thing. Usually it is someone looking to complain or an unsolicited salesperson looking to sell into the office. However, it could always be a potential new client. I am sure when the manager first started he would have come out of his office immediately to greet the person, as would be good business protocol. However, over time he probably got lazy and decided that he wasn't going to rush out to meet the unknown person in the lobby. When he finally did come out to see who was there for him, there was the CEO of the company staring him in the face. Apparently, the manager's lack of attentiveness to his visitor did not sit well with the big man.

Sometimes our lazy behavior and bad habits result in things that we can't as easily recover from and they leave more enduring scars. Unfortunately, today laziness, bad habits, and complacency are causing major problems across the board but especially on the roads. People are constantly playing with fire by trying to do so many things while they drive. They eat, they drink, they listen to music with their headphones on. I even saw a driver trying to read the newspaper. Of course, I haven't even gotten to one of today's major hazards which is texting while driving. Once you do these things a few times without any consequence, it becomes very easy to say, "it would never happen to me." However, a minor distraction at the wrong time usually ends up in a trip to the hospital, and that is your best case scenario.

So if you hear people say, "Why do bad things always happen to me?" it is most likely that they are lazy and eager to cut corners on everything in their lives and this raises the percentages that bad things will happen to them. Therefore, get in the habit of doing things the right way and being thorough in all areas of your life and "bad things" will happen to you less frequently.

CHAPTER 14

IT PAYS TO BE WELL-ROUNDED

From the early days of grade school, we learn that it is important to eat a well-balanced diet. A little bit of each area of the food pyramid is a good thing and an overabundance of any one segment is not. Life is no different. The most important thing I can stress to my children is to be well-rounded. We live in a society today that preaches specialization from an early age. Parents are encouraging their children to focus on certain skills and interests at disturbingly young ages. It is doubtful that a child is asking for this on his or her own at this stage; it is all the desire of the parents. A manifestation of this trend seems to be that a liberal arts education, which was once the norm, is now the focus of only a handful of elite colleges in the Northeast. Students are now graduating with highly specialized degrees with a focus on "hireability" especially in today's employment environment. This can be a shortsighted approach to your education especially if you don't go on to make a career out of your area of focus.

One of the most noticeable places you see this desire to specialize is in youth sports. Parents are forcing their children to focus on one sport or talent because we think it will perhaps lead to a scholarship, fame, or even a career. When I grew up we were all required to play a different sport every season and we wouldn't have it any other way. Nowadays, kids are being put on "travel" teams at the age of eight years old and being asked to focus on that sport all year round. While there are certainly merits to enhancing known strengths, we do this to our potential detriment. For instance, it is just as much of a learning experience to do the things that we are not as good at as the ones we are. It is important to challenge ourselves and learn to be resourceful. We must put ourselves in situations that allow us to learn how to not only be good leaders, but also followers. Life will put us in many situations that will take us out of our comfort zone and force us to figure things out. If we are only focusing on a small list of things that we already excel at, we will never develop other important skill sets.

A disproportionate focus on any one area of your life will eventually affect all other areas, including the one on which you were originally focusing. Just stop and look around you at those people who are one-dimensional. How is life working out for them? We all have at least one friend or family member who is a workaholic. Someone who is so caught up in what they do that their self-worth is totally dependent on their job title. The short-term benefit of this is usually a higher-than-average income level and a sense of power. The long-term effects of this, however, are usually a lousy relationship with family and friends, never mind a complete inability to cope once their fleeting success inevitably ends. So why would we encourage our children to focus solely on one area of their lives? The consequences are even worse at a young age because children don't have the same ability to speak up. The result is an eventual overwhelming sense of resentment. It may not come early but will surely rear its ugly head at some point. The crazy thing is, it even happens in that one percent of children who actually do follow through in this area of focus and become some of the top in the world at their craft.

The sports world is littered with examples of this. Andre Agassi was one of the world's best tennis players for many years and a very likable person. But he revealed in a surprising memoir after his career ended that he was never really happy playing the sport, even though he reached its pinnacle. He resented being forced to play tennis by his very controlling father. This phenomenon is not limited to celebrities. Our communities are full of local examples of parents putting immense pressure on their child to be good at something and forcing them to spend an unhealthy amount of time practicing. When that child grows up and does not fulfill the parent's vision, the result is usually a broken relationship between parent and child and often some sort of backlash behavior. You don't have to be a therapist to see this happening all around us. Just remember, the more pressure exerted on one side of the balloon, the larger the explosion on the other.

In my day, schools and parents focused more on developing leaders, as opposed to celebrities. Being "well-rounded" was something to be proud of and was stressed. Today, it seems like it is seen as a negative term. Almost a synonym for being average. As a youth, I was encouraged to develop as many talents and be exposed to as many cultures as possible. This thought has become passé because to do so would require time and energy that could be spent sharpening one defined skill. Today it is thought better to be exceptional at one thing rather than good at many.

The result is a complete dearth of leaders. In order to be a good leader, you must tap in to many competencies, handle various adverse situations, and see things from many different angles. Yesterday's leader has become today's highly trained expert. The thing is, leadership traits are timeless while specialized talents come and go. Once your trained expertise becomes obsolete or you can no longer execute it, you go back to being average. Leadership skills have no shelf life. Life is most certainly going to throw us challenges in all areas of our life, and they are not limited solely to the areas we are expert in. If we are not adequately prepared to deal with these challenges, it threatens the well-being of the whole. You are only as strong as your weakest trait.

CHAPTER 15

BEWARE OF THE PROUD PEACOCK

I have become increasingly wary of people who are insistent that I know something about them. It frequently turns out that these people end up being a far cry from the people they want me to think they are. In almost all cases, those that are truly talented or worthy of recognition let their actions speak for themselves. Conversely, whenever people let their mouths speak for them, it rarely speaks the truth. This person is often trying too hard to create an image of him or herself instead of letting us come to our own conclusions about who and what he or she is in reality. All too often it is a mirage, and the truth lies behind the image that we are being sold.

For instance, when I became the manager of an office of financial advisors, the first people that came in to introduce themselves to me and were seemingly going out of their way to befriend me usually turned out to be the advisors that I had to monitor the most. They would frequently come in to my office uninvited and tell me about their business and how they run it. They were trying to create an image of themselves before I had a chance to assess them on my own. Over time, however, the truth became apparent. If you have to rely on apple polishing, it is only because you don't have the skills to achieve the grades on your own.

Similarly, we have all been caught in those unfortunate conversations when someone is desperately trying to impress their importance upon us. They become professional name-droppers with the idea that their connection with these known people in some way validates their place in society. Conversely, in the 1980s sometime, my parents were invited to a dinner party. After my parents got home, my mother came to me and said that apparently she had sat next to someone famous at the dinner but was not quite sure what all the fuss was about. She wanted my help figuring out who it was and why everyone seemed to think it was so cool that she was sitting next to him. She was told he was a rock and roll star of some kind. I mentioned a bunch of names and she said that none of them sounded familiar. I was about to give up when she mentioned that he had big lips.

I said, "Was his name Mick?"

She said, "Yes, that's it!" Then she said, "What does that mean?"

I said, "Mom, ever heard of The Rolling Stones?"

In some higher-end neighborhoods, you can almost determine the worst cases of inferiority complex just by driving around town. The higher the gate at the front entrance, the worse the complex. Is there a legitimate security rationale for a twenty-foot, gold-tipped wrought iron fence? Someone should tell these people that in these situations most cases of robbery are inside jobs. Although something tells me the fencing was not erected solely with security in mind.

I am also wary of people who are overly verbose about their roles in charitable situations. Some people can do noble things occasionally yet do not live their entire lives in an honorable manner. Those of truly high character do a lot of good things every day but don't all wear this on their sleeves. Virtuous people perform honorable acts for their own internal satisfaction and do so without fanfare. They do not do so to try to influence the opinion of others. I have found that those truly comfortable with their place in society go out of their way to down play their standing. So what does this tell us about those that flaunt it? Beware of unsolicited information that people provide you about themselves. It can often be tainted.

CHAPTER 16

STOP TRYING TO GET EVERYONE ON THE SAME SIDE OF THE SEESAW

Don't expect everyone to have the same interpretation of an event as you do, because it rarely happens. Good leaders understand that almost all actions are seen through very different prisms. Therefore, reactions to what you might think would be straightforward events are rarely the same. Almost all actions have a buyer and a seller so to speak. For every person who likes the idea, there is usually one that doesn't. Every minute of every trading day, there are people buying a stock at the same time people are selling it. While you might think the terms of a deal are acceptable, there are others that feel they can do better.

People's responses to events and opinions are influenced by all sorts of cultural and behavioral factors. Combine this with the fact that there are a surprising number of people with behavioral issues, never mind the growing sense of entitlement that pervades society today, and it is a wonder anyone can have a rational response to anything. Therefore, as we go through life, it behooves us to understand that each person's biases cause him or her to see things in a way one might never have expected possible, causing totally unforeseen responses.

These types of unexpected reactions happen every day on very small levels. Sometimes these reactions can be caused simply by the intonation of your voice. For instance, the person you are addressing may not recognize your sarcastic tone. This occurs especially often in emails. Since tone and intent cannot always be ascertained in print, a simple email can be viewed through all different kinds of lenses. There are times when your attempts to help others might even be taken the wrong way and viewed with contempt. Especially today, when each community and workplace consists of people from all over the world from different cultural backgrounds, it makes sense to think through different possible reactions and understand that though you think you have figured it all out, there could be a reaction that you never imagined possible. Stop trying to get everyone on the same side of the seesaw. Differences in opinion are what make markets, so understand and embrace this and, when possible, use it to your advantage.

CHAPTER 17

A BIRD IN THE HAND IS WORTH... A BIRD IN THE HAND

I t is important to understand at an early age that when you get right down to it, all people are entitled to virtually nothing in life. If you start with this as a foundation, you will have a grounded perspective that will take you far. Much of the confrontation and stress that exists today can be boiled down to one simple thing—a distorted sense of entitlement. In this country, we are especially spoiled. We are very lucky as Americans to be entitled to "life, liberty and the pursuit of happiness" thanks to our forefathers. However, this is a pipedream in much of the rest of the world. As I see it, the only thing we are truly entitled to is to be paid for any work we have been contracted to do as long as it has been completed as outlined. We should be thankful for anything else. Yet some of society, especially in this country, walk around feeling entitled to a grand lifestyle no matter what has been done (or not, as the case may be) to earn it. Our country has become a grand welfare state and, as a result, we have morphed into a very complacent society. Without realizing it, we have created this trend through the "everyone wins" philosophy that has taken hold in our schools and other youth organizations. The idea of letting everyone feel good about him or herself is a noble intention and has its merits, but I believe it has gone too far.

I was watching my son's high school basketball game the other day when my eight-year-old daughter asked me when they would be giving out all the trophies. I had to explain to her that they did not give out trophies to everyone who plays in a standard high school game. After a long puzzled pause, she expressed her confusion as to what the point of playing was if there were no trophies involved. I had to explain that there were winners and losers. A concept today's youth is often shielded from. Young people today are sheltered from the realities of competition and failure until much later in life.

Certainly, entitlement is not a new phenomenon. When I was younger, I happened to be a decent tennis player. Nothing crazy, but certainly an above-average club player. One summer one of the mothers at our club went to the tennis pro and made her case that I should not be allowed to play in the tournaments anymore since I was much better than everyone else and was winning all of the events including the adult tournaments. It wasn't fun for the other kids anymore, she insisted, and it would be much better for the others if I was not allowed to enter. Instead of focusing on the process of simply playing in the event she was focused on the potential outcome and letting that determine her child's enjoyment of the event. Furthermore, instead of encouraging her children to improve their tennis skills to become more competitive, she felt it was easier simply to remove the best player from the event. It is no wonder so many people grow up with an inability to deal with the real world.

The last few generations, including mine, have not really ever experienced an earth-shattering event in the world (i.e., WWI, WWII, the Depression, etc.) that has served to reset the world's view on life. During the thirty-year period of 1914-1945, Americans were forced to live through incredibly difficult times in which people grew to be thankful simply to be alive and have roofs over their heads. The closest we have come to such an event is 9/11 and the 2008 financial decline. While significant events, as a country these events did not force us to endure intense day-to-day hardships for a period of several years. The downside of our country's sustained economic stability is an inordinate number of people who falsely believe that they are automatically entitled to a certain lifestyle. We all aspire to a positive place in society, but respect and success, like most other things in life, must be earned. Be thankful for all the very basic necessities that we all take for granted in this country and understand that you will need to work hard to achieve those things that you really want in life.

CHAPTER 18

HONESTY WILL SET YOU FREE

I am honest to a fault, although I am not sure there is such a thing. Telling a lie makes me terribly uncomfortable. The downside to this trait, other than making me a very bad poker player, is that it can sometimes be unnerving to others since, when asked for my opinion, I will always tell you how I see it or give you the facts as I know them. This can be unsettling to the recipient because it may at times come across as harsh. Furthermore, the truth can hurt, and many people don't live in reality. Some have also become affected by our overly politically correct world and will never say anything they don't think the other person wants to hear. I would rather say nothing than be dishonest or mislead people.

Some people tell lies; other people live them. They pretend to be something that they are not. They live lifestyles they can't afford, befriend people for the wrong reasons, and tell you they will do something they have no intention of doing. For the rational person, this behavior would result in intense anxiety. Trying to live a life not based on reality is incredibly stressful. As soon as you can, I urge you to figure out who you are, what you like to do, how you want to live your life, and then surround yourself with like-minded people. This will result in less anxiety, which usually translates to a longer and healthier life.

Ever notice that as people get older they focus less on how they look and what they do or say? It's because they just don't care anymore. They are tired of living a life of tension and aren't hung up on what other people think. They realize it is not going to affect them in any negative way. It provides them with a sense of freedom, as it is too tiring to live life in search of the approval of others. I am not saying to throw all sense of decorum out the window, but I am saying to stick to who you are at your core and be honest with yourself. Trying to be someone you are not will eventually backfire while also taking years off your life.

CHAPTER 19

THE CULPABILITY TEST

I consider myself a fairly good judge of character. I can pick up on little things about people that most wouldn't notice. Nevertheless, just like everyone else, I have been burned by people that I thought I knew. There are times when people seem to change and become completely different people overnight and sometimes your perception of someone shifts simply because you end up seeing them in a different light. In such a case, the person had these character traits all along, you just were not in a position to see them. Therefore, there does not seem to be any surefire way to screen people's character. I do know, however, that it is important to see people in as many different settings as possible before you make any strong determinations in regards to character. One's behavior can be different in various scenarios, and sometimes only certain people can see a particular side of a person. One's persona, for instance, might be very different in the office versus outside of it. Other examples might be treating friends differently than family or taking on a contrasting personality around superiors versus your peers.

Having said this, I have a few litmus tests that I have found to be good indicators of character. The first I call the "Culpability

Test." Simply put, are these people capable of recognizing when they are at fault and saying "I am sorry"? Sounds too simplistic. But, believe it or not, there are plenty of people that can never deem themselves to be at fault. No matter how much they are to blame, they find reason to blame others. They can completely reinvent events in their own mind so the fault does not lie with them. This fiction becomes reality in their brain, which is the scariest part of it all. Conversely, I have found that honorable people are more apt to take the blame for things even when it is not their fault just to keep things moving forward.

Another way to determine people's characters is how fast they repay their debts. Most people with strong values avoid owing people anything to begin with. However, on those occasions when something is owed, you can quickly determine what type of person they are by how fast they make good on their debt. These can be small or virtual debts like if someone picks up the tab for a dinner or if you lose a match on the golf course, etc. They don't have to be serious financial obligations. Those with weak character are always looking for handouts or coming up with some reason why they are entitled to ignore their obligations. Impressive people are rarely indebted to anyone, but on the rare occasions they are, they quickly balance the scales. As my stepfather always says, "Fast pay makes fast friends."

CHAPTER 20

UNDERESTIMATE NO ONE

I f you were to take a moment and look at all of the people that have come through for you in your life, my guess is some of the names on that list would surprise you. I have found that the people that end up making things happen for you are often those you least expect. Think of the people who have helped you find a job, supported a cause you have championed, done business with you, or come through in a time of need. Obviously, those closest to you, like family, usually do all that they can to support you. However, I have found that it is the people outside of this circle that often end up pleasantly surprising you.

This phenomenon became very apparent to me when I started my own business. The people that have gone out of their way to do business with me or introduce me to other useful contacts have consistently surprised me. I have my own unscientific ideas on why this is the case. I believe the answer comes down to a simple analysis of risk and return. My philosophy is that your best friends and contacts have already attained your friendship and trust. They don't really have to do anything at this point to increase it, and they don't want to do anything to jeopardize it. If they were to try to come through for you and fail, they might endanger your relationship in some way. On the other hand, if they were to help you by introducing you to their close contacts, they are risking their relationships with these people if you don't come through as advertised. However, someone that does not know you as well does not assume as much risk. That person is not jeopardizing a close relationship with you nor an established trust level. It is possible, however, that he or she wants to establish a better relationship with you, and by helping you can achieve this in a matter of months rather than years. Therefore, you just never know. Do not underestimate anyone's ability to impact your life.

Never burn bridges at any point in your life. This is especially true in regards to your career as industries are small and even when you leave a firm, some of these people may end up reappearing in your life. I am reminded of a team of sales people that left the firm I was working with and did so in a fairly flamboyant and abrasive way. They left to go to a competitor and, at that very moment, thought they were on top of the world and could afford to be a little brash. As luck would have it, a few years later their new employer merged with their old firm and, before they knew it, they were back working at the same firm as their old colleagues. Better yet, their office was assigned the same manager they had when they left, and you better believe he had not forgotten their previous behavior.

It is especially important to avoid overlooking others early in life. It is always amazing to look back on the people in your childhood who have gone on to be very successful. We tend to equate good grades, responsible behavior, and popularity at an early age with doing well later in life. Obviously, these are good traits and tend to be indicators of those who will go on to live decent lives. However, these are rarely the traits to look for in those that go on to be game changers. Those people that go on to be successful pioneers are often not the most responsible kids early in life. Trailblazers tend to live on the edge and often end up crossing the line. They have minds more apt to challenge the status quo, and they get so focused on their skill that it is not easy for them to fall in line. Big achievements usually require one to think way outside the box. I am not talking about slightly piercing the box, but rather smashing the box altogether. This can often result in many people writing these game changers off too early.

Furthermore, because they are usually not the most popular kids early on and can get reputations for being bad apples, they tend to be much more willing to assume risk later on in life. They have much less to lose, they have chips on their shoulders and are out to prove people wrong. In order to hit it really big, one has to assume a lot of risk. These young risk takers that hit it big end up being players in their community later on in life. The student who gets good grades and has a good great reputation growing up tends to play it safer and usually takes a more conservative path in life, like being a banker. Whereas the risk taker ends up starting a hedge fund and that same banker spends his whole life trying to get the risk taker to be his client. So here is the bottom line: treat everyone positively and equally throughout your life because, not only is it the right thing to do, but people and situations change, and you never know how and when someone is going to be in a position to impact your life.

CHAPTER 21

SPEAK SOFTLY...
LISTEN LOUDLY

Any student of history is aware of Teddy Roosevelt's famous motto, "Speak softly and carry a big stick." Well, I have my own version of this: "Speak softly and listen loudly." I have never been very good at doing this myself and, therefore, have become painfully aware of the ramifications of my weakness. I am very good at the latter part of the phrase—listen loudly—it's the "speak softly" part that always trips me up. I have never been very good at keeping my thoughts to myself. The downside of this flaw can be catastrophic. Having a strong opinion is fine. As a matter of fact, it is a critical ingredient to leadership. But you need to keep it to yourself unless absolutely necessary. Strong opinions, no matter how correct, are rarely positively received. Especially when younger and full of brash confidence, we can find ourselves with thoughts and opinions on everything. The world seems very "black and white" at this point.

When these opinions come oozing out at the office, you can get in big trouble. It can be a career killer. Here is what I figured out the hard way: no one at work really cares about your opinion unless you are the Chairman or CEO. Don't fall into the trap of thinking that they actually do. This advice of speaking softly translates to, "watch what you say, how you say it, and to whom." It is okay to have opinions, just don't present them too strongly. It turns people off, even when you are completely correct.

However, just as speaking too much can get you IN trouble, listening loudly can help you keep OUT of trouble and help you get ahead. Listening is a lost art. That is because it takes effort and energy. Letting other people talk and actually listening to what they have to say is not common these days. We live in a world of quick hits and attention deficit. Most people find listening tedious, but don't understand how much good information they are missing out on that could help them move forward. If done well, listening will help you notice things others don't, which gives you a huge leg up no matter what you are doing. When you don't listen properly, you end up giving people what they don't want or need and, as a result, you constantly miss the mark. Pay attention not only to what they say, but how they say it. Body language, facial expressions, intonations are all small but important things to pick up on in order to determine someone's intentions.

Now that I run my own company, I am always giving new business presentations. In these meetings, I have a short period to make an impression and succinctly explain the value of my proposition. Many times, I have to quickly get a sense of the people in the room as I am speaking. I try to determine what to stress, what to avoid, and generally how to steer the conversation. Recently, I was making a presentation and I noticed that the person I was presenting to was very fidgety during the meeting. I could tell by her facial expressions and body language that she was tensing up and getting slightly annoyed. She was looking at her watch, and I knew she was not at all interested in our services. My sense was that she felt threatened by what we did because it overlapped with her job at the firm. I sensed that she felt that if her firm used our company there might not be a need for her and she would not get credit for her work. Instead of seeing us as a possible valuable resource, she saw us as a threat. I, therefore, quickly changed my approach in the meeting and told her that our job was to make her look good in front of her colleagues. We would provide great concepts and access that would impress her teams and that no one even really needed to know how she was doing this. I explained that we could simply work behind the scenes if she wanted to and help her shine. Her demeanor changed on a dime. She perked up and all of a sudden wanted to get examples of good ideas that I could provide her. She ended up using our services. Sometimes you can listen with your eyes. The wise man listens while the fool is busy talking.

CHAPTER 22

SIMPLIFY YOUR LIFE

S implifying your life allows you to focus on a small list of things that are important to you and that make you happy. When you are spread too thin, nothing ends up getting done thoroughly and the result is a reduced sense of satisfaction. I am reminded of a trick thoroughbred racing trainers use on their horses. When trainers sense that their horses are too easily distracted coming down the back stretch, they put "blinkers" on their horses for the next races. These blinkers block the horse's peripheral view, which allows the horse to focus on the task at hand. The result can be a more determined and successful horse.

As we go through life, we gather all sorts of peripheral things in our life. We end up collecting random material items that usually end up in our closets and basements, but we also accumulate many other things that usurp our time such as causes, habits, and hobbies. When it comes to simplifying your life you have to start by determining exactly what makes you happy. When it comes right down to it, it is likely that only a few core activities make you really happy and give you a sense of fulfillment. It might not be clear at first what these things are, but your first step is to take the time to fully analyze this question. Chances are there are currently many ways you spend your time that don't really meet these qualifications. The suggestion here is to slowly minimize activities that waste your time and maximize the actions that truly provide a sense of fulfillment. I am not suggesting total elimination of these peripheral items, rather a slight readjustment of focus so that your actions and time are in alignment with your core values.

This process includes an analysis of the key people in your life with whom you spend most of your time. Surround yourself with those people that bring you happiness. Sounds very simplistic, but there are times that we might focus on people who are not constructive to our well-being and drain our energy. It is important to identify these people and reduce their role in your life.

The next step is to simplify your time. I am a fan of making long lists. I keep them on a pad on my desk, and each one usually has about twenty things of all kinds on it. However, it's very common to get sidetracked each day by projects that pop up and, as a result, not get to cross many things off of this list. As a result, at the end of the day there may be two items accomplished on your list, but a few other things have been added to replace them. The result is a trip home feeling like you have achieved nothing. I have learned to keep a very short list of key things to accomplish each day. There may be only two to four things on the daily "to do" list. I still keep a longer list of things to do, but I put it away and do not keep it in a prominent spot on my desk. I peruse this list and prioritize each day to come up with a short daily list. This is what I keep in prime view on my desk. Since I am not sidetracked by all the other items on the longer list, I zero in on my tasks and almost always accomplish all of them. This helps me prioritize and also leaves me with a better sense of accomplishment each day.

Finally, simplify your life by decluttering it. Get rid of all of the material things in your house that you do not need and which just take up space. If you haven't used it in the last five years, you won't need it going forward. Get rid of it. You can sell it and make some money or you can give it to those that are less fortunate. Both are fulfilling in their own way. This process may also include downsizing the house you live in. If the kids are out of the house and you are using half the space that you have, consider downsizing. This will eliminate the need to spend time and money on space that is not being used, including the outdoors. These actions, while difficult, will result in a reduction in your anxiety levels and an increase in your sense of fulfillment.

CHAPTER 23

NOT EVERYONE HAS A CALLING

I always envied those friends of mine that knew exactly what they were going to do when they graduated college. Either because they had a targeted skill that pointed them towards a certain career or because they had a future lined up for them through a family business, plenty of my classmates were zeroed in on a definite path. While I had absolutely no idea what I wanted to do for a living, these friends seemed stress-free and could focus in on sharpening certain skills. Thirty years later, almost all of these people are in the same careers they launched directly out of college. I had no obvious calling to a career, and that uncertainty created a lot of anxiety for me. It took me quite a while to figure out that the majority of people that graduate from college felt the same way. The liberal arts education I had received did not push me towards a certain career focus, yet most of my friends were driven, had defined skills and, as a result, were easily drawn to certain specific jobs out of college. This is a huge blessing, yet I am not sure they realized it.

I eventually realized that most people do not have one certain career that has been ordained for them. Very few people have a defined skill that will allow them to earn a living on that alone. The rest of us end up in careers more by accident than by anything else. I spent many years thinking that there was one career set aside for me and that it was my job to find it. We are programmed from early on to think this way. As a child, how many times were you asked, "What do you want to be when you grow up?"

Not all people are cut out to do just one thing during their career, and it could be that you are meant to have several different professions. This would allow you to take advantage of several skills, tap in to your creativity and, as a result, be more fulfilled. Because of my educational background and upbringing, I was fortunate enough to be exposed to many different potential occupations. There were several career paths I could see myself taking. However, I was so focused on determining the one thing I was meant to do with my life that I didn't try many of them. I am now running my own business in which I use many skills instead of one defined one. I am also writing a book and I am looking into a couple of other projects. I am no longer searching for that one career that has been put aside for me and am a much happier person as a result. So, if you are lucky enough to have a defined skill make sure you understand that this is a blessing. If not, try to take advantage of the fact that you are free to put your various skill sets to work in multiple work scenarios and realize that this is also a blessing in its own way.

CHAPTER 24

EVERYTHING HAS A PRO AND A CON

Most of the time, the downside or upside of our actions is so straightforward that the decision-making process is rather simple or automatic. In these cases, the ramifications are so clear that it is easy to determine whether we should or shouldn't do something. It's the decisions we make in which the pros and cons seem to balance out that are difficult to make. In these situations we often get blindsided by the pros and tend to minimize the cons. It is human nature to think that everything is going to come out positively and any risks we take will be rewarded. If this were not the case, there would be no lottery and every state would be bankrupt. I am not saying that we should not be positive thinkers for, as I state in Chapter 4, all great leaders must have immensely positive outlooks. What I am saying is that we should give as much thought to the downsides of our actions as we do the upside. The sexy stock we are looking to invest in has a lot of upside and could go up very fast in a short period of time. It can also cease to exist in a year or two and take with it the entire investment we have put into it. There was actually a time when some thought that real estate could do nothing but go up in value. It took a real estate bubble and a near-collapse of our entire financial system to dispel that myth. We must come to terms with any risks before we act and make sure we have a plan if things don't work out as imagined. I don't think this is done enough.

We have become a society that constantly searches for instant gratification. In the "old" days, it was conventional wisdom that you must work your way up a ladder and that all good things come in time. We were taught that we must educate ourselves and eventually acquire a defined skill that will serve us for our entire life. The path was traditionally to pursue a college degree and maybe even a graduate degree. Young adults would serve apprenticeships, clerkships and internships all in an effort to build an expertise that would establish a lifetime career. People were often employed by the same company for decades and were required to work their way up the ladder. How many times did I hear as a child the phrase, "In due time, son, in due time." Not today. We see tech companies starting up and, less than ten years later, being sold for billions of dollars.

With the advance of social media and Internet culture, we see people become famous overnight. There seems to be a pervasive thought process amongst the young that everyone is entitled to success, that it really shouldn't take that long and there doesn't necessarily have to be years of servitude to achieve it. For these people, the idea of dedicating yourself to any one thing for hours is hard enough to visualize, never mind a few decades. Nowadays, the value of a college education is even being second-guessed. Young adults see the rare and much publicized stories of Bill Gates, Mark Zuckerberg, and others who dropped out of college and became billionaires. The technology era has changed the way the young view their options as they start their careers. The cost of an advanced education today and the level of student debt has also had a major effect on people's decisions as well. While the near-term ability to taking a job that pays fairly well and avoid piling up debt seems tempting, the long-term effects of eschewing the acquiring of defined accreditations that can serve an entire lifetime are sizable. Most people are not going to build the next great thing or have the next big idea, and when reality sets in for these people they are usually already in a bad spot and their long-term chances of being successful have been severely affected.

This sense of entitlement and desire for immediate results has led to a lack of attention to the potential downsides to our behavior. We fixate on positive outcomes and, when they don't materialize, it usually impacts many other people in our lives as well. As a result, those closest to us are left to deal with our faulty short-term decisions and are usually left to bail us out when we need help getting on our feet. Therefore, ignoring risk is, in many ways, a very selfish act as well.

CHAPTER 25

FOR EVERY PEAK THERE IS A TROUGH

Most things in life have a cyclical nature. We think of cycles as things that only apply to stocks or the economy, but this is not the case. Many things that are out of favor at one point in time come roaring back in the future. Take fashion, for instance. My mother has kept almost every piece of clothing she has ever owned (at least the ones that the moths have not gotten to). She has even kept some of the clothes owned by her mother who passed away years ago. This is because women's fashion trends go almost as fast as they come, and they eventually come back into favor when you least expect it. My grandmother made a dress out of Lily Pulitzer fabric for my sister when she was about seven years old. Lily was all the rage back in the late seventies as was *The Preppy Handbook*. After my sister grew out of the dress, my mother kept it in her closet for forty years. During this time, the preppy look went dormant and all sorts of horrific fashion styles took its place like the hard to comprehend "grunge" look, for instance. Decades later my mother took that same dress out of the closet and presented it to my daughter when she was seven years old. It fit perfectly, had been preserved beautifully, and Lily Pulitzer and the preppy look had made a major comeback after going out of style for a decade or two. Now the preppy look is all the rage again as certainly demonstrated by the spectacular story of the Vineyard Vines brand. What goes around comes around.

I, myself, recently purchased a retro record player. I then went in search of a record store and bought some of the old albums I had listened to as a teenager. The sound the record player produces is totally unique compared to today's CDs or iPhones and listening to an entire album at once provides a totally different music experience. The record store owner told me that, after surviving a fifteen-year period when the industry became virtually extinct, business is now thriving as vinyl is now coming back into favor. Vinyl record sales have been steadily rebounding and have now returned to levels they haven't seen in almost thirty years. This recent phenomenon has sent me to the attic of my parents' house to find my old albums that had been left there a quarter of a century ago. I found them all, to my surprise and delight, and other than being covered in dust they were in perfectly good shape. When I brought them home to play on the new retro record player I had purchased, my kids sat in amazement. "This is how you listened to music when you were a kid?" they asked. I took a record out of the cover and gave it to them. They had no idea what to do with it, where to put it, or how to make it play music. They do now.

Just when you think things are dead, they seem to come back to life. The opposite can be true, as well. When something seems to have become the new paradigm, it often tends to come crashing down. Just look back at the tech crash of 2000 as an example. In the late nineties, as the technology revolution was just beginning, the stock market and particularly the NASDAQ took off. This period was exemplified by companies such as Dell Computer, Cisco Systems,

AOL, Sun Microsystems, Qualcomm amongst many others. In 1999, the NASDAQ rose over 80%, more than any major index in history. Qualcomm itself rose over 2000% in a single year. It is easy now to look back and identify the bubble, but It wasn't so easy at the time. Most young Wall Street "experts" were calling it a "new paradigm" and talking about why the old way of valuing stocks didn't apply anymore, trying to suggest that the world had changed. During the peak of the 1999 frenzy, I went to a dinner on Wall Street attended by some of the top financial advisors. The guest speaker was an old school Wall Street executive who was in his late seventies. The title of his speech was "The Dotcom Boom Will Bust." He spoke about how the current market valuations had no basis in reality and that the market would soon fall back to normalcy through a major correction. The sales people in attendance mostly discredited the words of the speaker, saying that he was too old and out of touch with how the new world worked. Within six months the markets had collapsed, immense amounts of wealth had been erased. Some of these "can't miss" companies even went out of business, and soon there was no more talk about new paradigms. The words of the old man turned out to prescient.

What goes up must come down, but it won't stay down forever. Therefore, never say never, because you just never know. Things have a funny way of boomeranging back in life. As a matter of fact, when everyone or everything seems to be pointing in one direction, it often pays to go the other way. Do not get fooled by extremes. It is okay to hop on bandwagons, just sit next to the edge in case you need to get off quickly.

CHAPTER 26

STAY AWAY FROM THOSE THAT BRING YOU DOWN

As I discussed in Chapter 11, we have the ability to control our list of friends. Friendships can and should be fluid, as we do not agree to lifetime contracts with our friends. Obviously, family is different. We don't have the ability to pick our family members, nor can we select our bosses. We do, however, have the ability to control whom we allow to impact our lives no matter how they became part of them. If you were to take inventory of everyone in your life, you would end up with a short list of people that make you happy, make you feel safe, and energize you. Just being in their presence gives you a positive outlook. Next, there is a long list of acquaintances in your life that are neutral. These are people who are not negative to be around, nor are they necessarily positive influences in your life. Finally, there will be a short list of those who bring you down.

It is hard to recognize these negative influences at first because they have been in our lives for a long time and we have just become numb to them. But if you give it some honest thought, you will realize that they are keeping you from reaching your potential. These are the people that you must keep at a distance. These might be family members, work colleagues, or lifelong friends. They are always negative, don't treat others well, have massive egos, or are compulsive liars. More importantly, they would have no problem taking you down to get what they want.

It is important that you find a way to reduce their impact on your life. Especially when we are younger, we tend to end up with more of these people in our lives because they may be very popular and it is hard to stay away from them when we are impressionable. As we get older, we may still hang on to these relationships because we lack confidence or we simply are unable to see the negative impact they have on us. In some cases, you can't avoid having them in your life, but you do have the ability to minimize their effect on your psyche. First you have to identify them, then reduce their role in your world while maximizing interactions with those that are positive influences. Subtle changes in who you surround yourself with can make a huge difference in your outlook and, therefore, your happiness.

CHAPTER 27

HITCH YOURSELF TO THE RIGHT STAR... BUT BE CAREFUL

Avoiding negative influences can impact the quality of your life, while maximizing exposure to the right people can be just as important to your success. Just like race car drivers or cyclists can "draft" behind front runners to help maximize their efficiency, you too can hitch yourself to the right person. Many a career has been made by aligning oneself with a person on the rise. Identify those in your world who are good role models, especially those that will be excellent examples in terms of work ethic and attitude. It certainly helps if their qualities have been recognized by their peers and are "moving up the ladder" quickly. Becoming a wingman to the right person can move you along quickly and potentially even result in you becoming the "top dog." Let's face it, we have all seen colleagues that have risen faster than others because they are close with the right people. There are many people that may have the exact same skills as you, but their abilities may have been better recognized because they more visible to key decision-makers.

Be clear, I am not advising anyone become a "yes-man" to anyone. No one likes a yes-man, and it is easy to identify them. They do not have a mind of their own and provide no value themselves. They are simply there to kowtow to their superior and stroke their ego. I am, rather, advocating finding a mentor that you can learn from, bounce ideas off, and get help making big decisions. This person can be anyone you know. Having a mentor is important in all aspects of life, but it especially helpful to have such a person in one's earlier years.

As a high school or college student, having a mentor or surrounding yourself with the right people can have a major impact on your success. It is not necessarily important to align yourself with those with the most impressive skill sets, but rather those you can best learn from in terms of work ethic, resourcefulness, positive attitude, and creativity. Good mentors with these attributes can shape your life for many years to come.

However, this piece of advice comes with a warning on the label, which is to make sure that you do not attach yourself so closely to any one person to the point where you become totally reliant on him or her for your existence. It doesn't matter who the mentor is or how positively this person is viewed by others. First, it is important that you develop your own set of skills in order to survive over the long-term. Secondly, you must develop your own mindset and values in order to be true to yourself. Finally, if something negative happens to the person you have aligned yourself with, you don't want to go down with the sinking ship. The wind can change rather quickly at large companies. Power struggles are a common occurrence, and it's not always the "right" people who survive. When senior-level person is removed, it often leads to a purging of those that are part of his "team." You don't ever want to put yourself in a position to be part of the residual damage of these structural changes. I have seen many people rise quickly only to be gone when their "star" burns out. So find a good mentor in life, but be your own person and develop skills that make you essential no matter who is in charge.

CHAPTER 28

BE BEHOLDEN TO NO ONE

When I was a teenager, my stepfather and I would make a one-dollar wager on the Monday Night Football games. It didn't matter who was playing. The goal was simply to make the games more interesting to watch. Believe it or not, a dollar is all it takes to pique your interest. Neither one of us could ever stay awake through the end of the game. As a matter of fact, we could only make it to halftime. Yet, the next morning, if my stepfather had lost, there would be a dollar bill sitting right outside my door. He would leave it there on his way to work. It was always there if he lost. I used to say to him, "You know, you don't have to pay me when you are heading out the door at the crack of dawn. You can pay me later." To this he would respond, "Fast pay makes fast friends." So, obviously, I had to be ready to pay him in the same manner on those occasions when I lost.

Similarly, my mother used to sit down at the end of each year and figure out who my parents "owed" from a social standpoint, meaning people who had invited them to something to whom they hadn't yet reciprocated. They would then throw a year-end cocktail party and invite everyone that made that list. So I grew up with a strong sense of never wanting to be in debt to anyone.

There are three reasons that you never want to feel like you owe anyone. First, how it makes you feel; second, how it reflects on you; and, finally, how it may affect your decision-making going forward. The most obvious and direct way to be indebted to someone is to have taken a loan from them. However, there are many other small situations that may cause you to feel like you owe a debt to someone. For instance, when you go out to dinner and someone else pays the tab, when you play golf with someone as a guest at their club, or when you are invited to an event to which they have obtained the tickets. These are all seemingly small debts, which are not necessarily to be repaid directly, but understand that when people do nice things for you, you should find a way to repay them or make sure that you acknowledge the kind act. For example, if you ask your friends to support a charity or cause of yours then you need to be prepared to support theirs when the time comes.

It would be a mistake to think that these things are not noticed. There may come times when people will try to sway you. Either because they want to be your friend or because they want you to become a client. They will go out of their way to do things for you, invite you to things, or send you gifts. If you have no intention of reciprocating in these situations, make sure you do not accept the invitations in the first place. You never want to hear those dreaded words: "You owe me one."

For example, I was putting together a foursome to play golf a few years ago and contacted an acquaintance of mine to see if he wanted to join us. Our sons played on the same travel baseball team, but I was also trying to establish a business relationship with his firm. He declined my invitation to play by saying that his company had yet to do business with me and, therefore, he didn't feel right accepting such a nice invitation. I explained that the invite did not have to do with business and that I would simply enjoy playing with him. Nevertheless, he said, "When I am in a position to do business with you I will gladly accept the invite." I understood and respected his response. He did not want to feel awkward by accepting an invitation that he could not repay or that might affect his future decision-making on business matters.

Now, I am not saying that you shouldn't ever let someone do something nice for you, as this is the way the world works. Hopefully, you are a nice enough person that people will be willing to go out of their way for you. However, I am saying that you do not want to be a taker. You never want to put yourself in a position where people feel they "own" you. When this happens, your decision-making can become affected and you can wind up in awkward situations or doing things simply because you feel you have to. There are people who go out of their way to create these situations. They want to give the impression they can exert power over you. Because of their status, power, money, or job title, they will do something for you simply because they have something in mind that they want from you. Generally, you can spot these people from a mile away, but you have to keep your guard up because there are other times in life that this manipulation can be very subtle.

CHAPTER 29

SOMETIMES THE FAT LADY JUST DOESN'T SING

The most famous visual I have for celebrating an outcome too early has simply become known as "The Play." This took place during the 1982 football game between the University of California and Stanford. Stanford was led by the immortal John Elway at quarterback and had taken the lead with four seconds left on a field goal. All that remained was the kickoff to finish the few seconds that were left on the clock. Stanford kicked off to Cal, who started to pitch the ball around in a series of laterals trying not to get tackled. What made the scene even more unbelievable was that the Stanford band, assuming the game was over, stormed the field as presumed victors in the annual rivalry game. However, unbeknownst to them, the Cal players were still successfully running the ball back and, with the band on the field, the players maneuvered the ball through band members all the way in to the end zone for a touchdown to win the game. The Stanford band was completely unaware and on the field playing their fight song in celebration. Defeat had been snatched from victory. The other event that makes my point, of course, is the famous 1984 Doug Flutie Hail Mary pass to beat University of Miami with no time on the clock.

The sports world is full of examples of seemingly miraculous events, but there are many instances outside of sports as well of calls made before all the results were in. There was the 1948 election of Dewey vs. Truman in which the newspapers printed the infamous headline, "Dewey Wins," assuming a Dewey victory at press time. Maybe it is because I am a real sports fan, or to be more specific, a Mets and Jets fan, that I have always been extremely cognizant of counting your chickens before they hatch.

I have had many instances of absolute certainties unraveling in my own life as well. After graduating college, I went into the sports marketing business. My first real sports job was working for a triple-A minor league baseball team in Oklahoma City. After a year of doing this, I applied for a job with Major League Baseball. I was called in for a series of interviews, and the likelihood of landing the job was looking very good. I was to hear something any day. Labor Day weekend approached, and I called the office to ask if it was okay for me to go away for the weekend on a planned trip to visit a friend on an island, as, once there, it would be difficult for me to get back quickly. I was told that they had no issue with this since nothing would be happening for a while and certainly not over the long weekend. So, off I went. I was right in the middle of my round of golf on one of the top golf courses in the country when a car pulled up. My friend's mother got out and told me that they had taken a phone call at the house from MLB needing to talk to me. I ran off the course and called the office with immense anticipation. They told me that they needed to meet with me as soon as possible. I explained that I was away for the long weekend, that I was on an island and, furthermore, that I had called before I left to make sure it was okay to do this. I also explained that I did not have a suit or any business clothes with me. They said they understood and to get there as soon as I could. So I borrowed a blue blazer from my friend, got on the first ferry off the island and made the long drive to New York City. I met with several people and was told everything was looking very good and to go home and wait for a call.

The call never came. As a matter of fact, no communication of any kind ever came. I tried calling my contacts there, and no one would take my phone call. I was completely dumbfounded. What had happened? My mind started racing, and I wondered if I had blown it by not having a suit for our last meeting even though they knew the circumstances. This was not it. All that had happened was a case of extremely bad timing. Just about the same time I was interviewing with the league, the famous Al Campanis television interview on *Nightline* took place. Al Campanis was a Los Angeles Dodger executive who was being interviewed by Ted Koppel for the anniversary of Jackie Robinson's integration into baseball. Well, as luck would have it, Mr. Campanis made some racially charged comments on the air which started a whole firestorm about Major League Baseball and race. The result of which was an examination by the press of the lack of minorities in key positions in the sport. Mr. Campanis was fired, and it was suggested to me that this event affected how they would need to approach the hiring of this position. Let's just say they definitely went in a different direction when they eventually filled the position.

This new job was all but in the bag. Any rational person would have chalked this one up in the win column. This, however, is not my style, as the true pessimist in me always assumes something bad will happen. I have a hard time accepting good news even after it has been confirmed for a long period of time. Of course, the above story doesn't help me with this as I am often reminded of it just as things seem to be signed, sealed, and delivered.

When I started my own business, I encountered many examples of things falling through at the last minute as well. I was counting on one new client to be the foundation of the business and allow me to get started. A friend of mine had brought me in to meet with his company. He really liked the services we were offering and decided that we could help his team. I had several meetings with them and many specific discussions about what we would do for their company. With this seemingly in my back pocket, I felt comfortable going ahead with my business concept. I quickly incorporated my business and focused on finalizing everything with my first client. I drafted proposals while also putting together everything needed to open the business. It was at this point that my friend at the company resigned from the firm. I had no idea this was happening. I followed up with everyone else we were talking to there, but there was no longer any appetite to move forward with us. The main driver of our opportunity had left. I had just incorporated and now the piece of business upon which I was going to build my company did not exist. I ended up starting my business anyway without a signature client. Actually, without any clients at all.

A few years later I was working on an athlete endorsement project. I was orchestrating a deal whereby a client of mine was going to endorse a very young golfer who had just turned professional. He had not made the PGA Tour yet, but was full of potential. This was going to be his very first endorsement deal. We were towards the end of finalizing the contract. At this point, I reached out to the golfer and made sure he was fine with the parameters of the deal and was ready to move forward. The next step, I explained, was meeting at the client's office to meet the key people in person and review the agreement. He agreed and we set up a time to meet. He arrived at the meeting and we went over the details. He met with the top people and even took some pictures with them. The meeting ended positively, and all that was left was for him to sign his first ever endorsement deal. It never happened. He went home and, about a week later, left a voicemail late at night stating that he did not want to sign the agreement. During all this, he had apparently been talking to some other people who were telling him they could get him a better deal. We never heard from him again.

There are certain moments or periods of your life, both professionally and personally, when certain things seem inevitable. Something may seem like a "sure thing," but it is important that we try not to see things this way. Because if we do, we inevitably move on mentally to other things and take these outcomes for granted. This may potentially change our behavior and cause us to do things we might not otherwise do. See everything through to its very end for, as I am sure you have learned by now, there is no such thing as a "sure thing."

CHAPTER 30

NEVER BET ON THE PACESETTER

I n horse racing, there is usually a pacesetter in every race. A speed horse that gets out to the front and sets the pace. It quickly jets out to the lead and usually has a few horses chase him. These horses are always impressive out of the gate and initially look unbeatable. The thing is, though, these horses almost never win the race. They eventually tire out, and so do the horses that have been chasing them. This leaves the door open for the other horses that have strategically placed themselves and remained patient to come storming from behind and win. Life can be very similar sometimes.

I try to go back to my high school reunions when possible and am always amazed at who shows up to these events and, more importantly, who doesn't. All of the people I figure will be there often don't end up being in attendance. Most of the really popular kids in the class don't come back. The ones who do are usually the lower profile people. For a while, I figured it was unique to my school since I went to a boarding school, but I don't believe it is. My general theory is that many of the most popular kids in high school were at their peak at that moment in life. That was it for them; they peaked in high school and never quite reached those levels again. They do not want to come back to see their classmates again because they think it would change our image of them for some reason. What makes a teenager popular is usually not what makes an adult popular. As we mature, the attributes we look for in friends and peers evolve. Go back and look at your yearbooks and see who was voted "most likely to succeed" and see how many actually did. While they seemingly got off to a fast start, they may not have looked so impressive in the later furlongs of life.

In football, an underdog might take an early lead and look prime to pull the upset. But usually, the better team makes adjustments and, over time, their skill, preparation, and coaching leads to a victory in the end. In politics, the new candidates usually start with very high poling numbers because very little is known about them. Once their backgrounds are revealed and the media starts testing them, those numbers usually start falling. This is why politicians carefully time when they announce their candidacies. The 2008, 2012, and 2016 Iowa Caucuses were won on the Republican side by Mike Huckabee, Rick Santorum, and Ted Cruz respectively. But these pacesetters eventually ended up at the back of the pack.

The same can be true at times in business and in the workplace. There is often one employee within a department that seems to be on the fast track. He or she gets in early and leaves late, has a big personality, never sits down, and talks often of big accomplishments within his job. However, I have found that, over time, these employees are prone to fizzle. They are often doing all of these things because that's all they've got. They rely on visual effects to make impressions. While this behavior is often pleasing to their bosses, in the end, results are what matter and often those who produce results are the ones that are less obvious at first glance.

We are often fooled in life by early impressions. But it is important to understand that patience, commitment, and intelligence are all things that allow one to be successful in the end. It takes commitment to follow through on a project completely and to eventually "raise the trophy" so to speak. Getting out to a fast start is great and better than the alternative, but it can sometimes lead to a sense of complacency. Most people have a period in their lives when they seem to be at their best and their skills and personality traits lead them towards being complete people. You never want to peak too early. Understand that most of the time talent, hard work, and preparation prevail in the end. For all these reasons, it is important to know that you must never give up on something. Stick to a game plan, be thorough in everything you do, see things through, and usually you will accomplish your goals and be recognized by others over the long-term.

CHAPTER 31

LEARN TO HIT THE CURVEBALL

There are many talented baseball players in the country some of whom go on to play minor league baseball, but only a very small percentage of these ever see a pitch in the major leagues. One of the key differentiators between a minor league player and a major leaguer is the ability to hit the curveball. Most top players can hit a fastball no matter how fast it is thrown, but only a few good hitters learn to hit the curveball well. These players are the ones that move up to play in the big leagues.

Life is no different, you will be thrown many curveballs. In order to be successful in life, you have to be able to handle these unexpected developments. In the short term, you must be flexible enough to expect everyday surprises and handle them with a sense of calm. This comes from understanding that surprises are the norm. Simply realizing this can help you react to change in a professional manner.

There are two types of change that you must prepare to handle. First, there are the daily surprises that we encounter that require us to adapt and change course. Things like an employee quitting, a key player on your team getting injured, or a job transfer. These events demand short-term adjustments on your part. Your positive reaction to these events and, when possible, the ability to turn a negative into a positive will determine your success and happiness. It is not the event itself, but your reaction to it. Then there are the seismic shifts that take place in life. The permanent very long-term changes that require holistic adjustments in the way you view the world. These are things like changes in the competitive landscape of your business, divorce, a death in the family. Your appropriate reaction to these events is necessary in order to maintain your current quality of life.

All generations have seismic events that shape lives. Previous generations had such cataclysmic periods as the Depression and World War II that intensely affected their lifespan. 9/11 was such an event in the less distant past. We are also currently living through a technological revolution. This has completely changed the business and social landscape of our time. This revolution has brought change to many industries at lightning pace. The business world is full of companies that had difficulty adapting quickly enough to the competitive landscape. Kodak, Blackberry, AOL, the entire U.S. auto industry are a few examples. Apple is a terrific example of a company that didn't adapt, almost went under, and then, through management change, adapted in such a positive way that it reemerged as the dominant pacesetter in the entire industry. In order to respond positively to change you must expect it and always be looking two steps ahead. Those that achieve this not only survive, but thrive.

CHAPTER 32

RESIST THE PATH OF LEAST RESISTANCE

Electric currents follow the path of least resistance. It is not necessary for you to. It is very common to see people take the easiest path toward achieving something. As we will discuss in the next chapter, this should not be confused with swimming downstream. There is a big difference between going with the flow and being lazy by choosing the easy way out. Many people get too focused on the outcome and not the process and, in so doing, hurt themselves in the long run.

An example of this can be seen in people's pursuit of education. Some students focus on attaining their diploma but don't really care about the path they take to get there. When I was a freshman at Yale, I had to choose my major. I ended up choosing one of the "easier" options. Everything is relative because there is no such thing as an easy major at Yale, but in the world of higher education I choose a major that would be considered taking the easy way out. I regret this decision to this day. I had the chance to really better myself, and I don't feel that I took full advantage of the opportunity. While I achieved my goal of earning my diploma from Yale, there were different roads I could have taken to get there.

People also cut corners on their health too. In order to lose weight or increase their energy they choose diets and regimes that certainly may achieve their short-term goals, but may affect their overall well-being in the process. I once had a friend that lost twenty pounds in two months on a low-carb diet. He was eating bacon burgers and eggs every day and dropping waist sizes every week. While the immediate benefits of looking good on the beach are hard to ignore, the long-term risks associated with this regime are at least worth discussing especially when you consider the founder of this type of diet had a heart attack later in life.

Today's technology has given us the ability to choose the easier path every day. It has become commonplace to hide behind email, social media, and texting both at home and at work to try to make our points. Instead of picking up the phone or writing a note, it has become easy to avoid handling difficult situations directly.

There are many different ways to get something done. The path you choose will determine how and if you will build character and impact other people in the process. In many cases, taking the long road will be tougher, but your journey will result in building a stronger foundation for yourself and will allow you to better deal with difficult situations in the future. It is important that you challenge yourself at times and take assignments that test your boundaries. Success in these cases will build confidence, while failing will build character. People underestimate the benefits of failing especially early in life. Therefore, don't be afraid of encountering resistance and confronting your outer limits. All good leaders have been battle tested.

CHAPTER 33

SWIM DOWNSTREAM, NOT UP

I t is important not to get this confused with taking the path of least resistance. Taking the path of least resistance is a conscious decision to take the easy route as opposed to the more challenging one when there is a clear difference in the potential benefits. Swimming downstream or "going with the flow" refers to the conscious choice not to stand in the way of something on which you would potentially take a different approach because you realize that you will most likely not be able to change the overall outcome. The tricky thing about this is realizing that you can't or shouldn't change the outcome. Better put, the energy you would need to change the course being taken does not warrant your effort. A simple cost-benefit analysis has occurred in this case, if perhaps unconsciously. Swimming downstream in this context is generally a good thing while taking the path of least resistance has a negative connotation.

I am a big proponent of going with the flow, although it took me half my life to figure out its benefits. When I was younger, I did not have this foresight. If I did not agree with a method or felt a different approach would be better, I would speak up, make my opinion known, and try to affect the outcome. As I got older and wiser, I realized there are many instances when it is best to just be quiet and let it all play out. It is not that you have gotten soft, it is just more of a realization that you have to pick your spots. If you choose to fight city hall on everything you feel isn't right or that you disagree with, you will run out of energy and accumulate unnecessary stress. I am not suggesting lying down and being a pushover by any means. What I am preaching is to factor in the impact on you and those around you when considering how to react in these situations.

There are several places in your life where this strategy is most beneficial. The area in my life where I became most familiar with the benefits of swimming downstream was the handling of my divorce. For those of you that have been through this process before, you know that there are a million instances when you could choose to argue over what you feel is not fair. This is true especially during the actual divorce proceeding and for years to come if there are kids involved. The process of dividing assets and handling the time with your children results in constant small negotiations. The meteor shower of contentious issues causes the rational person to realize that the effects of arguing over all of them would be catastrophic, not only to you but, more importantly, your kids, new spouse, and family. Therefore, you have to learn to bite your lip and let the little things go. You are calculating that the benefits of doing so will be the right choice for all areas of your life on a long-term basis. The irrational person feels that he or she needs to argue over every potential negotiation point no matter how large or small and doesn't seem to be able to see the negative effects of his or her actions.

You and your spouse will both have quirky little things that will drive the other crazy. In most cases these hot buttons are trivial, but you learn that for some reason they are important to the other person. My wife, for instance, thinks that I am completely incapable of doing laundry. It is her fear that I am going to ruin any and all loads that I do. She has, therefore, informed me of her desire to have me refrain from going near the washing machine. Now most men would find this punishment more than agreeable. However, I have reminded my wife that, given the fact that she is twelve years younger than I am, I have been washing clothes quite successfully since she was in grade school. This reasoning seems to have gotten me nowhere. I run my own business and have a home office. Therefore, I pass by the laundry pile several times a day. In an effort to help out, I often put a load in the washing machine when I see the need. This attempt to be productive has gotten me in nothing but trouble. Every time I do so, even if successfully avoiding turning everything a different color, I get nothing but an earful. So eventually, I had to heed my own words of wisdom and go with the flow. I have gone against my innate instinct to be a dutiful spouse and decided to stop washing anyone's clothes.

I got better at going with the flow when I came to understand that not everything ends up 50/50. Not all things end up being exactly fair. Sometimes you get the short end of the stick and it's not worth fighting for the longer one. Irrational people think they deserve the longer stick in every single case. They will expend the energy to fight for more than their share in all instances. They develop a bad reputation, wear themselves out, and end up very unhappy. My advice is to save your energy and resources to focus on the things that are most important in your life. Try to think big picture and focus on a small list of major things. Understanding that you won't always get your way or your fair share, you will live a longer and more fulfilled life.

CHAPTER 34

TIMING IS NOT EVERYTHING, BUT IT IS A MAJOR FACTOR

Hard work, dedication, and skill are major factors in getting ahead and becoming successful. However, almost all successful people can point to some case of very good timing that played a major role in their success. Good timing can often be considered the result of a very wise, educated decision or a keen understanding of probabilities and risk. Other instances of timing are pure luck.

In a previous chapter, I told you my own story of how timing had impacted my life in the case of my potential job with Major League Baseball. However, as for many of us, this was just one of many instances in which timing may have affected my future. Another of these occurred when I was about eight years old. My father took my sister and me to London during our summer vacation. We arrived at the hotel, and it was time to go to sleep. I have never sleep walked before and I haven't since, but I did on that fateful night. As a child, I had a recurring nightmare that the Russians were bombing (I am a child of the Cold War). Well, on my very first night sleeping outside of my home country, I had the dream again. This time, I got out of bed and proceeded to leave the hotel room, the door locking behind me. I got on the elevator and went down to the lobby floor. I walked through the lobby, which was full of people checking in, and started to exit the hotel. All of this was taking place while I was sound asleep. I was an eight-year-old boy in my pajamas about to walk the streets of London. As soon as I exited the hotel, I woke up. I shudder to think about what might have happened if I had woken up even one minute later. I had no idea what hotel I was in nor where I was. Thankfully, I did wake up and made it back safely to my hotel room.

Luck and timing are often major factors in the careers of successful executives, athletes, and entertainers, among others. My stepfather, whose nickname is "Stretch," fought in World War II and then went on to be a successful executive on Wall Street. He has many stories of luck and timing. During the war, he fought in the Hurtgen Forest in Germany, which was one of the most dangerous assignments in the war. A bomb landed in his foxhole, killing his radio man, but miraculously sparing him. Somehow he survived this and made it to V-E Day. Still enlisted, his division was set to be deployed to the war that was still going on the Asian front. However, his division never had to go off to fight in Asia because of Harry Truman's decision to drop the atomic bomb. This ended the war against Japan without my stepfather's Division being deployed. Yet, years later, in researching where his Division was set to have been based and what their assignment was to be, he learned that in 1945, a devastating and deadly tsunami had hit the exact place he was to be based, killing most people in its path. So, had the bomb not been dropped, he would have most likely perished. The timing of Truman's decision was a twist of fate that surely saved his life.

He went on to a career on Wall Street and took a job at Reynolds Securities, which was, at the time, a top regional financial services firm. After some time there, he felt the company was not being run well, so he decided to leave the firm. He went in to the boss's office and handed him a letter of resignation. His boss looked at it and asked if he had presented the letter to the CEO of the company. He answered that he had not, but that he would give it to whomever was required. His boss told him that he couldn't resign without giving it to the CEO personally. To this day we don't know if that was accurate or just something his boss told him to buy some time. So, Stretch took the letter and marched over to the office of the CEO, Tom Staley. Meanwhile his boss got on the phone and called Tom. He said, "This employee of mine is on his way down to your office to resign, but we can't afford to let him go."

So, when Stretch walked into the CEO's office, Tom said, "I understand you want to resign".

Stretch said, "Yes, sir."

"Well, tell me why you want to leave"? he asked.

"I don't feel like this firm is being run well, so I am going to go to another firm," Stretch responded.

Instead of throwing Stretch out of the office and saying good riddance, Tom asked him what they could do to improve the firm. After Stretch's response, Tom asked Stretch to stay and help him fix the firm. Long story short, he accepted the offer and stayed. Tom Staley and Stretch Gardiner went on to be great friends and, years later, Stretch ended up right where Tom was, as CEO of the firm. He went from resigning to staying at the firm that he would one day run. Most any other time, when one submits a letter of resignation saying you don't feel like the firm is as good as it could be, your letter will be gladly accepted and you will be shown the door. This wasn't one of those times.

These are just two stories of timing and luck that played a major role in one man's life. However, timing plays a role in everyone's life, so never be ashamed when you are the beneficiary of good timing. The world is littered with people who have suffered bad luck and timing, so it is better to be on the right side of that trade. If Stretch hadn't been a well-respected employee, Tom would have thrown him out of the office. So just remember, you can put yourself in a better position to be the recipient of good timing and luck through hard work and honesty.

CHAPTER 35

BEWARE OF HUBRIS

The taller the cliff climbed, the larger the potential fall and the smaller the chances of survival. As one ascends the ladder of success, the more cutthroat it gets and the greater the risks of a catastrophic descent. Sometimes this occurs due to ignorance, occasionally laziness is to blame, but most of the time, the cause is hubris. The source of this hubris may be wealth, power, or fame. However, success only exists in your head if you let it. Whether you are captain of your high school football team or MVP of the Super Bowl. Whether you are a state senator or US senator, whether CEO of your home business or CEO of a Fortune 500 company. Success is all relative. If you are a big shot in your own world, no matter the level, hubris lurks as a threat to your current standing in life. The key is to never see yourself as "successful." Once you see yourself as being in some way different from others, entitlement creeps in and ego is not far behind. If ego sets in, it changes the way you see the world, and your sense of reality starts to dissipate.

In some communities, a net worth of a half a million dollars will put you on the top of the food chain. You will see yourself as better than others. Yet, if you lived in a different town, you might be living in a dwelling designated as low-income housing. It's all relative. Obviously our world history is full of leaders, politicians and celebrities that have fallen victim to their egos. Thankfully, more than any other country, the U.S. embraces success. Our country is built on the dream of doing well and the rewards that come as a result. However, we also have less tolerance for those who abuse this success. It doesn't take much to fall to the bottom. People like nothing more than to find a good reason to knock others off their pedestals. We applaud people that make the effort and become "successful" at something. If their falls are due to bad luck or timing, we have no problem with it. We also have no issue with people who are simply not very good at something. We applaud the effort of trying to succeed. Yet, if this failure is caused by hubris, we tend to have little tolerance, and shame will often fall upon your effort.

To avoid this pitfall, it is important to avoid letting hubris become part of your world. The key to this is all in your mindset. The average schoolteacher or nurse, for instance, does not normally achieve wealth, fame, or power through their occupation even though they may be the very best at their craft. There are not any red carpet award ceremonies on television recognizing the work of the best teachers or nurses in our communities, though there should be and you don't usually find them to have intensely large egos. Being the best at something selfless, like these professions, should be no different than being the best at something that does bring fame and fortune along with it. Always understand that your standing in your own community is not a given. It can disappear in an instant. Humility is the key to maintaining long-term success.

Second, avoid people that have fallen victim to ego because they will eventually fall and, if you are too close to them, you will be caught up in their avalanche. There are many people who feel they are important not because of what they do themselves, but because they are close to someone who is deemed important. They work hard to become part of that power player's "entourage" or associate themselves with them. This is all great while that person is still in a position of power, but once the star falls from grace they are left to be shoved aside. The next time you start thinking that you are something special, just think about this: unless you are someone that will be read about in our history books, about a year or two after you have passed away, you are on the minds of only a handful of living people and about ten years after you have gone, there is virtually no one that even knew you existed. It doesn't matter how much money you had, what your title was, or what kind of power you wielded while alive.

CHAPTER 36

OPTICS MATTER

When I graduated from Yale, I initially had no idea what I was going to do for my first job. I wanted to get in to the sports marketing business, but had no real connections to the industry. Of course, most of my friends were off to Wall Street or law school, and the more creative ones sought work as writers or something similar. So there were not many Ivy Leaguers out pounding the pavement for sports marketing jobs. I did, however, have summer job experience on my résumé having worked in minor league baseball. I just scratched and clawed my way into interviews wherever I could get them. These interviews did not go well at first. As I look back now, I can understand why. I was pretty bad at interviewing at first, like most people fresh out of college. I thought that if I put on a nice suit and handed potential employers a résumé listing an Ivy League diploma I would stand out. Well, I did stand out, but for all the wrong reasons.

I had a nice Brooks Brothers gray pinstripe suit with some sort of power tie (the Eighties were all about the power tie). This look was great if you were trying to become the next Gordon Gekko, but not so good if you were looking for an entry level job in sports.

Make no mistake, I was getting my chances, I just wasn't making a good impression. I ended up interviewing directly with some of the biggest names in sports at the time. People like Frank Cashen, the general manager of the New York Mets, and Mark McCormack, the founder of IMG and the sports marketing industry himself. I am sure that interviewers saw the Yale degree and the pinstripe suit and thought, "This guy is in the wrong place." Because I was not able to definitively verbalize my commitment to getting into the industry and my willingness to start at any level, they made an assumption that I would not be willing to do the grunt work that it took to get your foot in the door. Of course this was not accurate, but I could not initially overcome the quick judgments that were being made based on how I looked and where I had gone to college.

Eventually I had to just get any job I could find. I saw some information about a job opening as a paralegal at one of New York's most prestigious law firms and set up an interview. I went in with the same résumé and the same pinstripe suit. The interview took about thirty minutes and, at the end of the interview, they asked if I could just stay and start right then. True story. I was going to make some pretty good money and work as a paralegal on one of the most high profile cases in Wall Street history, the Michael Milken case. So, after countless great interview opportunities in the sports marketing industry with nothing to show for it, I got a job offer in thirty minutes at one of the top law firms in the country. Why do you think this is? Because optics matter. People make extremely quick judgments about you before you even open your mouth. It shouldn't be that way, but it is. Once these judgments are made, it becomes your job to live up to them or, at times, overcome them. In the case of the sports marketing interviews, the initial judgments were negative. Yet, in the case of the law firms, they were positive.

These quick assumptions are being made about you all the time in all aspects of your life. When you sit in your classroom as a student, your teacher is making judgments about you simply by where you sit, your eye contact, and how you behave. Are you taking notes furiously or looking directly at the chalkboard with a focused look? Or are you in the back of the room looking disinterested? Teachers are more apt to give the former person the benefit of the doubt on his or her work, the latter less so. By simply putting some effort into how you look and what you wear and putting a smile on your face, positive assumptions will be made about you. It doesn't always mean they will be correct, but just be aware that these snap judgments are being made and you have control over them.

If you are walking in for a job interview at a bank with a nose ring, what do you think the interviewer is thinking? Why not just take it out for the interview so you don't have to overcome these assumptions. It's okay to leave it in, but then don't whine when you don't get the job. Many times you control these optics. Sometimes you don't. There was a great baseball player for the San Diego Padres and New York Mets in the late Eighties by the name of Kevin McReynolds. He played center field like it was effortless. This worked in San Diego; it didn't in New York. Even though he was an all-star player, he never received the appreciation he deserved in New York because he was so smooth in the field that it looked like he wasn't hustling. This was, of course, not the case, but it's how it looked to the fans. In New York there is no greater sin as an athlete than looking like you aren't hustling. He was being punished for being too smooth, simply because of the optics. I am not suggesting you avoid being yourself, for this is imperative. Just be aware that optics matter in how people perceive you, so work them to your favor.

CHAPTER 37

SOMETIMES YOU JUST HAVE TO ROLL THE DICE

I am, by nature, a fairly conservative person, but sometimes in life it makes good sense to roll the dice. It is very difficult, at times, to receive great returns without assuming some risk. This doesn't mean that it shouldn't be a calculated risk. The key is to make sure that the ultimate downside is not going to put you out of business, so to speak. Every decision you make entails a cost-benefit analysis by you. Most of them are made in a split second, but some need to be well thought out.

As previously mentioned, after college I was working as a paralegal simply to make a living. I was working with bright people, but the work was more than a little mundane. My real interests were still in trying to find a job in sports, so I kept an eye out for opportunities in that industry. One day, as I was sitting in a room full of people filing, I realized that the baseball winter meetings were taking place in Dallas. This event is the annual gathering of all the important people in baseball. Owners, general managers, and league executives all met once a year in a convention-like setting. I had an epiphany that I should try to go to these meetings to try and find a job.

Since the meetings were starting in just a couple of days, I figured there would be little chance of finding a room in the exact hotel the event was taking place, even though it was the largest hotel in Dallas. I called the hotel and they said there was one room left but it was a suite. In a bold and spontaneous move, I took it. I called American Airlines and reserved a flight and then proceeded to print out fifty copies of my résumé. Since I had worked in minor league baseball, I knew maybe one or two people who might be there, but that was about it. I had no real plan, I just grabbed my résumés and flew down, figuring I would walk around for the weekend and see if I could land a few interviews or meet some key people.

When I got to the hotel, the place was buzzing. A massive hotel full of important people in the baseball industry. I checked in to my palatial room and just started walking around the hotel. There was one room dedicated to job opportunities in the industry—sales people for teams, radio and TV broadcasters, ticket office personnel, etc. However, I eventually learned that many of the jobs available were not posted. The teams just filled them themselves by talking to people they knew.

I ran into one of the two people that I did know at the convention. Granted, I didn't know her very well, but amongst a sea of unfamiliar faces she was a welcome find. She owned a Triple-A team located in Oklahoma City called the Oklahoma City 89ers. She told me that the team hired six interns each season. These people did absolutely everything. They were hired to sell anything they could: season tickets, advertising, billboards, promotional nights. They also helped out during games, worked on PR, painted the bleachers...you get the drift. They were "gofers", but I didn't care, it would be a great foot in the door. She introduced me to the general manager of the team as he did the hiring for these positions.

I told him I was interested in talking to him about an internship position. He looked me up and down and said in his best Oklahoma accent, "Okay, boy, meet me in my room at halftime of the game tonight, I will give you a few minutes".

The game he was talking about was a college football game, and the one thing I knew was you did not mess with men from Oklahoma and their college football viewing. So, I sat in my room watching the game and, as soon as halftime came, I ran down and knocked on his door. I came in and he sat and looked at my résumé. I knew I only had as long as the halftime intermission lasted, so I had to work fast. He would alternate looking at my résumé and taking a glance at me. Finally, he said, "What on earth does a boy that graduated from Yale want to work in minor league baseball for?"

I am quite positive whatever my answer was did not quell his concerns. Yet, after pausing for a minute, he said, "Any guy with an Ivy League degree that is crazy enough to come down here in search of a job must be serious about it." He then proceeded to offer me one of the internship positions. I was to report to Oklahoma City in three weeks. My foot was in the door.

CHAPTER 38

IT TAKES MANY YEARS TO BUILD A REPUTATION, BUT ONLY A FEW SECONDS TO RUIN IT

You start building a reputation for yourself at a very young age. We begin labeling kids when they are as young as seven or eight years old. We will quickly define them through very simplistic descriptions like, "He is the smart one," "a handful," "a piece of work." Many times, as we get older, we become aware of these labels and may even unconsciously mold ourselves to match them. I am not a psychologist, but in many small acts throughout our lives, how we carry ourselves, where we go to school, we create a reputation for ourselves. Sometimes good, sometimes not so good. Sometimes accurate, sometimes not so much. Many people keep the same reputation forever, some change it, some run from it, and some spend their whole lives trying to live theirs down or overcompensate for it. Therefore, the first thing to understand is that you start making deposits in your reputation bank at a very early age.

It was no different for me. As a youth, I had no interest in trouble. I didn't like it, didn't like people who did, and I steered very clear of it at all times. It didn't stop me from having a lot of fun. I just made sure fun didn't turn into trouble. Hard to do, but it can be done. For those that didn't know me very well, I ended up with the reputation of being very serious. I was an average student until I went away to boarding school where I hunkered down and became one of the top students in my class through nothing but sheer hard work because I was certainly not blessed with a brilliantly high IQ. I then got into an Ivy League school, which can certainly impact people's impressions of you.

In my high school and college years, I had several friends who were not exactly choir boys. Sometimes I lived vicariously through them. Parents would sometimes hesitate about their child going out at night with this group, but they would say, "Well, if you are going out with Stuart, it must be okay." They could go out as long as I drove.

Eventually your label becomes a heavy backpack. It can be a burden at times, even if a good one. Your reputation takes many years to build and should be valued at all costs, because once it is lost, it becomes difficult to get it back.

These days with all the new technology, a reputation can be lost in an instant. I am seeing this happen more and more with the youth of today. They have no sense of the dangers of the Internet and social media and do incredibly stupid things with this technology that can never be erased from their résumés. I can't imagine the trouble some of us would have gotten into in our youth had the Internet been around. Since the beginning of time, young people have done stupid and mean things as they learn how to mature. However, today their stupid acts are captured by a camera or a website for all the world to see. I have seen kids' reputations damaged before they even reached college.

When I grew up there was a premium put on privacy. These days there is none. If you are not on a social media outlet sharing every little thing about your life, then you are seen as the outcast. Kids these days have no notion that the picture they posted of them in a bathing suit with a beer funnel in their mouth will be viewed by their potential employers. This one picture will speak more about their employability than four years of getting good grades will.

It's no different with adults. Somehow they believe that posting pictures of themselves at very fancy resorts or at some amazing vacation spot will somehow make us view them in a positive light. They don't think about that one email they sent at work that was inappropriate or rude. Email these days blows up more careers than any other thing.

There are many examples of people whose reputations were seemingly ruined overnight, but in reality, they behaved like this for many years and no one knew. Bill Cosby, Lance Armstrong, and Bernie Madoff are good examples.

The infamous story of Lance Armstrong is a particularly disturbing example of a reputation imploding because, in this particular case, so many people worldwide had invested personally in his story. Lance Armstrong was, by all accounts, one of the most successful American cyclists of all time. However, he was diagnosed with a serious case of testicular cancer in 1996. He fought and won his battle against the disease. He then formed a foundation dedicated to cancer survivors. The foundation went on to be named the Livestrong Foundation and eventually became a phenomenally successful worldwide campaign with Nike. After his scare with cancer, Lance went on to win seven Tour de France titles, surpassing any and all accomplishments before his cancer. His story was so unique that it inspired people around the globe and resulted in Livestrong becoming one of the most successful charitable campaigns in history. After his first Tour de France win, allegations of doping by Armstrong started to emerge. These rumors did nothing but intensify after each Tour win. Lance vehemently denied all of these stories and sued publications that issued stories on the subject. He tried to take down anyone that was tied to these reports. There was only one small problem and that is it turns out they were true. He eventually admitted to some of these allegations and was stripped of all of his Tour de France titles and banned from the sport. This case of a fallen hero was particularly upsetting because people around the globe had bought in to his story of perseverance through their support of the Livestrong campaign. He played with our emotions.

Reputations are damaged on the local level every day as well. Sometimes you can actually get your reputation back, but this requires one simple act of courage that many are not willing to take, which is to admit your faults and apologize. Americans are very forgiving, but they require those simple two words to even begin to think about letting you off the hook and move on. A good example of this is legendary radio host, Don Imus. Let me start by saying I am a big fan of his show, which has evolved immensely through the years. One day he made a very stupid comment on the air. I am sure it was meant to be funny, but it didn't come off as such. He lost his job over it and many years' worth of good relationships. But he realized he had made a mistake and, instead of hiding from it, he owned up to it. He personally met with the people he had offended and apologized face to face. It took a few years, but he is now back to where he was before the incident.

Your reputation is built through your daily actions that serve to define your character. How you treat people, respond to events, and carry yourself all help to determine how people view you. Through the repetition of small things you do every day, you create an image of who you are. Don't blow it all up with some stupid act without thinking.

CHAPTER 39

NEVER TAKE FOR GRANTED THE CHIPS YOU HAVE ALREADY WON

I t is human nature to want more of a good thing, whether it be wealth, friends, customers, power, or acclaim. Once we gather a noticeable amount of these things, we tend to focus on securing more of them. There is absolutely nothing wrong with this goal, unless we neglect and, therefore, jeopardize what we have already secured. There is always a point of diminishing returns no matter what the quest. We get so focused on what we don't have that we completely ignore what we have already achieved and secured. We start taking things for granted, and soon they start to disappear.

Let's take wealth, for example. Almost everyone desires more money. Many people have enough money to live a decent life. Certainly not all, but many. By decent, I mean they can feed themselves and put a roof over their head. There are some people who are fortunate enough to be able to do a lot more than this. Yet many of these people still don't feel satisfied with what they have and feel like if they only had more money their life would be better. They take for granted the wealth that has already been secured, and they spend it at a very fast pace. Feeling entitled to a certain lifestyle and attempting to keep up with their friends results in their treating their wealth as if it will always be there. But like a sugar addiction, spending money makes you want to spend more, and the cycle becomes hard to stop. This is all fine until one unforeseen incident changes your world.

We see it all the time in the sports world. Young athletes that make an unusual amount of money after never having any. They see the amount they are currently making and quickly adopt a fantastic lifestyle. Problem is, they are not thinking about a lot of things they should be. For instance, the average lifespan of their career. It is often very short for professional athletes, so they must make their entire life's earnings in just a few years. They are not thinking about life after their career. As a result, they spend what they are earn and when the merry-go-round stops, they have nothing to fall back on. For example, NBA star Antoine Walker made over $100 million during his career and ended up filing for bankruptcy just a few years after retiring from the game. He went on to work with current players to help them try to avoid the same fate. The other thing athletes don't think about is risk. They assume that no injury will greatly affect their earnings potential and lifespan. The result is a number of former pro athletes who end up with nothing to show for their careers after several years of being out of the business. They did not respect what they had already achieved and took it for granted.

Same thing with business owners. Many businesses focus very well initially on securing clients or customers. They provide good service and a positive experience. The clients initially feel appreciated and receive a lot of attention. But then, in their quest to grow the business, business owners turn their attention to bringing in new clients and customers to make the business grow. For the original clients, the calls stop, the attention dissipates and, eventually, better and bigger clients are brought aboard. The feeling of being appreciated goes right out the door and eventually so do those first clients. The business turnover rate begins to skyrocket, and it therefore becomes necessary for the business to keep finding new clients to replace the ones that leave. They become a mouse chasing its own tail.

I am a sports fan and watch a lot on TV. I chose my television provider because it has incredible sports options. I have been a good customer of this company for twenty years. However, in the company's drive to find more customers, they always offer special deals to new customers. For instance, offering packages that I have been paying full price for to new patrons at a discount. This does not sit well with me as it is customers like me that have allowed them to build their company. We should be the ones getting a special deal, not people who have never bought their services before. Build from within and watch the results grow.

I saw many examples of this over thirteen years working in the financial services industry. As a manager of financial advisors, I would watch these advisors focus on bringing in new clients while, at times, ignoring the ones they'd had for years. They would stop making proactive calls to a client and then be angry and confused when the client would leave. They ended up taking these customers for granted. Focus on the clients you have, pay them attention, and you will have them forever and, as a result, more will come in through referrals. It feeds upon itself. Focus on your core or, as they say in politics, "play to your base" and you will always be in a position of strength. Always respect what you already have in hand. Start with your family and work your way out.

CHAPTER 40

YOU ARE MORE ADAPTABLE THAN YOU THINK

L ike animals, we humans adapt to our environment. It is a survival mechanism, just like in the jungle. The problem is we downplay our ability to adapt and tend to avoid it at all costs until it becomes necessary to survive. How many times have you heard someone say, "Well, I could never..."? Any of these phrases sound familiar?

"I will never be friends with that person"

"I could never live there"

"I could never think like that"

"I could never do that job"

Yes, you could. You could do any and all of these things if your situation changed or if you simply allowed yourself. At some point in your life, your situation will change and the result will be an adjustment in the way you view the world. My stepfather is now ninety-four years old. In his day, he was an immense presence at 6'7" and an extremely confident man. There was a day when he used to say that if he was ever in a position where he couldn't take care of himself he would pack up his bags. He couldn't imagine ever being in that position. Well, he had a serious stroke on the night of his eighty-ninth birthday and now lives with a caretaker 24/7. He relies on his caretaker for almost everything, and it doesn't bother him at all anymore. He is very happy. Life has a way of changing your perspective in a hurry.

There have been many times when life has taken me to new places that required me to adapt. As mentioned in a previous chapter, early in my career I took a job working for a minor league baseball team in Oklahoma. For me, living in Oklahoma is just about as close to the definition of a fish out of water as you can get. I am a WASPy Ivy League graduate who bought his first pair of jeans when he was twenty-five years old. If I could, I would have worked out in my khaki pants. So the idea of my living in Oklahoma was intensely amusing to all those who knew me. However, it wasn't long before I was accepted by my colleagues, and I grew to love their Midwestern honesty and values. Years later, my career took me to California where khaki pants were the equivalent of wearing a tuxedo. I am most likely the only person to have lived in the Golden State for more than a year without ever having been on a surf board. I could not ever get used to watching NFL games at a sports bar at 10am, and there is something deeply wrong with watching football over eggs and bacon. Yet I absolutely loved my time there. I appreciated the sun being out every day and the ability to be active all year round. I ended up moving back to the East Coast, underwent a career change in my early thirties and started a new job on Wall Street. My office was in the Twin Towers. I am not a morning person to say the least. Unlike most people, my most productive time of the day is the afternoon and evening. Getting to work by 9am and being productive in the early hours has always been a challenge as it takes a while for my engines to fire. This is not a good match for finance. The bad news about my new job was I had to be at my desk by 7:30am. Furthermore, I lived out in New Jersey, and it was an hour and a half commute to the city. This meant I had to get up at 5:00am and be out the door by 5:40am every morning. For most people on Wall Street, this is no big deal, but to me it was life changing. I never thought I could do it, but the thing is when you get yourself into a routine you start to adjust to your new reality, whatever it is. Your mind adjusts along with your body and, pretty soon, you have established a new norm.

Of course my examples of adapting are extremely minor. Franklin Roosevelt literally woke up one morning and his once vibrant legs didn't work. He went to bed a healthy energetic man in his prime and woke up a victim of polio. This is an example of extreme adapting. He went from being a vice-presidential candidate to being bed-ridden and having an uncertain future. As is human nature, he adapted to his new norm. He bought a mineral water site (then thought to be a cure for polio) and invited people from all over the world to come out and try to be cured. He went from circulating with the most important people in the world to hanging out with invalids in a pool. He brought hope to many people, including himself. He changed the way he viewed the world and went on to become one of the most influential presidents in our history. His story can be used as an example in so many of the chapters of this book. If you come to terms with the fact that when one door closes another opens, it will alleviate a lot of your stress about change. Something always fills the void as long as you allow it.

CHAPTER 41

DON'T EVER TRY TO PUT A SQUARE PEG IN A ROUND HOLE

I n your effort to improve things, never try to put a square peg in a round hole. It never works over the long term. You might be able to get away with it for a while, but over time, the faults will be exposed. People everywhere are under duress to make things happen. At work, at home, in your social network, the desire to become a "player" is felt by many. Especially these days of very low attention spans, people's patience levels are limited. Many people feel the urgency to make it happen today, not tomorrow.

This lack of patience leads to very poor decision-making which can reveal itself in many different ways, such as makeshift policy, unwise mergers, products that are faulty, purchases that one can't afford. Some companies get stuck on a huge merry-go-round. The turnover at senior levels is so high that there is never such a thing as a long-term strategy. New management is always looking to make its mark. They don't want to maintain the status quo and, therefore, often make changes just for the sake of it. People today are constantly looking to make a name for themselves. Many times this leads to attempts to reinvent the wheel. They take something that is working fairly well and has been proven over time and try to completely revamp it instead of making minor adjustments.

In my lifetime, I actually saw an historic instance of this up close. During the summer of 1985, I took a summer job working on the floor of the New York Stock Exchange. This was back when they still had "specialist" firms that acted as the go-between for every trade. They were the ones that actually made the market for particular stocks. Nowadays, it is all computerized. During one slow summer day down on the floor, something unusual happened. All of a sudden, a group of traders started running towards our trading pit. A frenzy ensued of traders selling shares of Coca-Cola. Each specialist firm had a list of stocks that they were responsible for making a market in, and the one I was working for traded stocks like Coca-Cola, Johnson & Johnson, and other big names. So if you wanted to buy or sell shares of Coke you had to come to this trading pit to do it and, on this day, everyone was there to sell. There was not a buyer to be seen. This meant the specialist firm had to make the market and buy all of those shares. We were so busy trying to fill the trades that we did not know why this was happening, and this was long before the days of Internet and smart phones. After the trading day was over we soon found out what had caused all of the selling pressure. Coca-Cola had come out with a new version of the famous Coke formula. They called it "New Coke." It was a flop. No one had any interest in a new version of what was, most likely, the most famous and successful consumer product line ever created. The stock price plunged, management was criticized, and New Coke was pulled from the shelves not soon after. This is now a case study in business schools all across the country as an example of management trying to make something happen just for the sake of it. There was not a lot of great rationale for messing with a phenomenally successful product. When something is working, stick with it. Instead, focus on places where things are clearly not working.

We see examples of companies making irrational decisions all the time. Many times company politics plays a part. They will put people into management positions that don't make sense because it may be an easy way out of a problem or because they simply don't want to make a difficult decision. They will remove a senior person from their role and, instead of letting them go, they will simply move them into a different position within the firm, often a role they are ill-suited for. They can get away with these strategies for a while, but eventually this person will create issues in his or her position because he or she does not have the skill set to deal with it, and will be exposed. All the company has done is kick the problem down the road.

Examples of forcing the issue do not stop at the office. We do it at home as well. Parents will put their kids in positions that they know are most likely not the best for them simply to satisfy their own vision of what they want the child to do. We see this with sports and extracurricular activities. Parents may push a child to play a certain sport because they played it in their youth or because it is the popular thing to do within that community and brings the parent a certain amount of social standing. The parents want to be a part of the social group that is created by the sport and make their children play, whether it is something they even want to do or are best suited to play. The end result is usually a child who ends up resenting their parent and eventually moving away from the sport.

People at times also make irrational decisions when it comes to saving money. They want something but can't really afford it, so they try to get away with doing it cheaply. It never works. A friend of mine was doing some work on his house. Nothing too major but complicated enough that doing it yourself was not worth the time or effort. Now, this person happened to be very handy, so you would think he would make the right choice when it came to who would do the work. But he didn't. He chose someone that gave him a very low bid for the work. He paid the contractor a deposit, and the work started. All was good. Eventually the work stopped, the contractor said he needed more money to complete the job, and when my friend said he had already paid him what he said he would do the job for, the contractor left and never came back. The work wasn't even close to being done, the contractor had left with his money, and my friend was left to finish the job himself. Shortcuts never work out. Do the job when you have the money to do it correctly and not until then and don't ever try to cut corners. It always comes back to haunt you. Make the hard choice up front instead of trying to make something out of nothing or forcing something to work that isn't a right fit. Finally, keep in mind that sometimes the right (though difficult) choice is to not do anything at all.

CHAPTER 42

PATIENCE PAYS

Haste definitely has its place. For instance, if your teenage daughter is trying to get tickets to the just announced Taylor Swift concert, it is best not to mull it over for too long because they will sell out in a matter of minutes. If you are a technology company trying to get a new product to market, time is not your friend. However, for the majority of projects and goals, it pays to be patient.

I am always intrigued by the long lines of people who stand in the cold to be the first to get a new hot technology gadget. They are so focused on being the first one in their community to say they have it that they are willing to pay literally double what the rest of us will pay when the price inevitably drops on the product a year later. As a matter of fact, over the long run patience will save you a lot of money. The stock you wanted to invest in that has been going up every day will most likely take a breather at some point and come back down to you; your dream house will usually turn up if you just keep looking; that outfit will go on sale if you can only wait until after Christmas. In most instances, time is your ally. The seller is banking on your inability to show any restraint and to catch you in the heat of enthusiasm.

Patience pays off in all aspects of life, including one's career. I have discovered that in the workplace, especially at large corporations, no one really likes colleagues that are too brash. Management wants you to think outside the box, they just don't want you to step outside the box. The eager beaver and the know-it-all don't last long in the corporate environment. How many times have you seen that employee who seems to be everyone's newest golden boy? You and your colleagues, however, see a different side of that person. You see major weaknesses, and you all say to yourselves, "What on earth do they see in this person? He is not what they think he is." You are tempted to say something to someone and try to point out the issues. Never a good move, because in the long run, most of those golden boys end up getting what they deserve. It takes time, but after a while the cheese falls off their cracker and their weaknesses are exposed.

When I started my company, I met with a senior person I knew at a large financial firm. I made a presentation about the services of my new company. He really liked what I had to say and told me that he thought his firm could benefit from our services. He then introduced me to the department manager who oversaw the type of things we did. I was asked to put together some concepts on a project they planned to do. I worked very hard to put together a great presentation and proposal. I thought all was going well until, one day, this point person at the firm told me point blank that there was no way I would end up doing any work for the firm. She made it clear that she oversaw everything that happened in this area and she was not going to let me and my firm do any work for their company even though I had come to her through a senior executive there. She went on to say that she didn't want the firm doing any business with anyone that overlapped with her responsibilities and that she wanted to make sure that there was no chance her bonus could be affected by what they might pay my company.

She felt intimidated by my company's capabilities and basically told me, "Not on my watch." She thought that if the firm liked what I was presenting that it would somehow reflect negatively on her. She was afraid her bosses would say, "Why haven't we seen this type of thing from you?" The bottom line was, she worried that if they hired me to do what she did, she might lose her job. She wasn't confident enough to allow us to make her look good in her role at the firm. So, I was in a very awkward position. This department manager was a good friend of the senior executive who had brought me in and was enthusiastic about my firm's services, but she was telling me on the side, "It's not going to happen." She went so far as to tell me not to contact any of the other people at the firm anymore. I was torn. Do I say something to the senior person about this behavior or do I just go quietly on my way? If I go quietly, the senior person would wonder what happened.

After a lot of back and forth, I decided not to say anything to the senior executive. I knew the time I had put in on this was a waste because she was going to bury all of our work. But, I decided, I could wait out her tenure. If I was patient, time was probably on my side. I figured that, over time, her behavior would show itself and she would not be in that role anymore and, therefore, it would not make sense for me to say anything to the senior people. Five years later, I was sitting at a bar having dinner with some friends when the senior person at that firm who had originally brought me in sat down on the bar stool next to me. After some small talk, he asked me about my business. I told him it had grown and was doing well. He said, "You should come back in and meet with us again.

The department manager who you had been talking to is no longer with the firm. She was let go."

A few days later, he sent an email to connect me with that person's replacement. I was back in talks with that company. It took five years, but my patience paid off. I went in to meet with her and, a few months later, they called me in to discuss business opportunities.

Patience pays off in sports all the time as well. How many times have you seen the big underdog get off to a fast start in games and look like they are going to pull the upset? With adrenaline running through their veins, they are playing above their skill level and look great halfway through the game. Yet, in the second half, the better team stays the course and eventually pulls it out in the end. The veteran coach does not panic. He sticks with the game plan and knows that in staying the course, talent will eventually take over. It is the coach that overreacts to the initial developments that ends up losing to the inferior team. How many times does the horse with the early lead win the race? Very rarely. The experienced jockey remains patient, sits off the pace, and waits for his opening to break through. The premiere running back strings the play out and waits for his hole to open. The batters in baseball who can't touch the hot pitcher wait him out and are patient. They study his pitches, delivery, and timing, and this often pays off in the latter innings. Patience is a virtue, as they like to say. Stay the course and good things will happen. Over the long term talent and truth usually trump all other cards.

CHAPTER 43

HEDGE YOUR BETS

I have stressed that every decision you make has a pro and a con. It should, therefore, be easy to recognize that it is necessary to hedge your bets when possible. There is a time to passionately invest in something, to make a bold move, or to believe in a cause. However, it is always necessary to have a backup plan. There is not a legitimate financial advisor on the planet that would tell you to invest all your money in one stock. We are taught to diversify our portfolios. Life is no different. The world is full of instances of things not turning out exactly how we would like them to. Furthermore, as we get closer to a situation, we tend to be blinded by our passion and see things in a distorted light. It becomes harder to see the truth.

Our country was founded by people taking risks and passionately following their dreams. It is necessary to stick our necks out at times in order to be successful and reach our goals. However, we must always make sure that we invest only an amount of resources that, if lost, still allows us to survive in a meaningful way. Resources can include money, assets, reputation, time, and energy. We must ensure that we will not be wiped out personally, financially, or mentally. There are hundreds of people who invested with Bernie Madoff who would support me in stressing the importance of this. Many people gave Mr. Madoff all of their money because their belief in him was so strong. Looking back, it seems easy to find the fault in this, but at the time there was no reason to think that these people were putting their future at risk. Mr. Madoff seemed to be a major pillar of the community and a highly accredited person in the money management industry. His bio was impressive as was his list of clients. As a result, these people trusted him and put all their eggs in his basket. A move that turned out to be disastrous. We have all learned since this infamous story broke, that it is wise to diversify advisors just as much as it is investments. Unfortunately, this is not the only recent story of people or institutions turning out to be very different than we imagined, as described in Chapter 38.

It is wise to hedge your bets at the workplace as well. I have seen people attach themselves to executives on the fast track. They try to establish themselves as wingmen, so to speak. With this they enjoy the same quick rise up the ladder that their colleague does. It is all a rosy picture until they get higher up the executive ladder where the oxygen gets thin and things get cutthroat as there is only so much room on the top of the pyramid. There are often major power struggles resulting in a clear winner and loser. However, if a mentor losses the power struggle, so do all of his mentees. To the victor goes the spoils, and that includes the right to get rid of anyone that was part of his adversary's team. So it is wise, at work, to diversify your support amongst many people. Do not invest completely in one person. The ride up can be fast, but never as fast as the fall back down.

It is healthy and necessary to make commitments in life, however, it is just as important to have an exit strategy. Before, you make a big decision, ask yourself what the world will look like if it doesn't work out the way you envision it. It is not necessary to assume the worst-case scenario, but it is wise to understand it.

CHAPTER 44

BE KNOWN FOR WHO YOU ARE AND NOT WHAT YOU DO

Y ou can learn a lot about life by attending funerals. First, the person whose entire self was tied to what they do for a living, usually has a very nice casket and very few people there to see it. Conversely, those that were known for who they were as opposed to what they did usually have a modest casket seen by many. Second, I have never attended a funeral where a person's title was even mentioned in the eulogy. Attending funerals puts a lot of things in perspective. You live your entire life interacting with all sorts of people and, in the end, these people make a decision as to whether they should attend a one-hour ceremony to commemorate your life. Their decision is entirely based on how you treated them and impacted their life. If the answer is not positive in either case, chances are they would not cross the street to attend your funeral. Have you ever stopped to think about who would attend your funeral if it were held today? It might change the way you approach life.

If your whole self is wrapped up in what you do for a living, the people in your life will be made up almost entirely of people who want something from you. Depressingly enough, this can sometimes even include your family. In this case, since they are not your focus, you most likely don't have much of a relationship with these people and your main use to them is in what you provide them. The remora fish is a very small fish that has dorsal fins that act like suction cups. These allow them to attach themselves to other larger fish such as sharks or whales. Remora fish can swim on their own, but they use the larger fish to provide transportation and protection. They also feed off of the remnants of the larger fish. Make no mistake, we are all surrounded by such remora fish. People who rely on us to survive. These people could care less about us but are very interested in what we offer.

If you are someone who focuses on being known for who you are, you are usually surrounded by people who are interested in you as a person, and they really don't care about what you do. They value your relationship and sustain it by returning the support and friendship they receive from you. This type of person can have a very successful and fulfilling career but see employment as simply a way to provide for themselves and their family. They enjoy their work, but don't let it define them. They receive just as much enjoyment from the days they are not in the office as the days they are in it.

However, there are other types of people whose entire persona is defined by their career and the power, control, and attention it brings them. These people are the ones you see with their titles or jobs featured on their license plate. You know the type. What these people don't ever seem to understand is that there will be a day when their job won't be there to define them, at which point they will crumble. When I was in the sports business, I ran into a lot of these people. One particular acquaintance of mine had a very high profile job in this industry. He was constantly interacting with sports celebrities and attending high profile events of all kinds.

Furthermore, since it is such a glamorous business, people in these positions often receive a lot of attention from people who want to get into the industry. But one day he was suddenly let go from his job, and he never recovered. His entire identity was wrapped up in what he did, and he didn't have anything else to fall back on when he needed it. He never really found another job and his personality was never the same.

On the other hand, I once asked a former CEO of a Fortune 500 company what part of his life he looked back on most fondly. I figured his answer would have to do with some part of his very successful career. It did not. He said, "Right now, I like today, being retired." That's the difference. Warren Buffett strikes me as one of these people. The richest man in the world and the best on the planet at what he does yet his identity does not seem to be entwined with his work. He has no interest in proudly displaying his success in business, which is supported by the fact that he has lived in the same house for about sixty years and now has given most of his wealth to charity through the Bill and Melinda Gates Foundation.

There is one notable exception to the rule and that is the very small percentage of people on earth whose entire being is wrapped up in what they do because they are literally changing the way the world works forever. They are focused on something that is going to change society and how we live day to day. These people live and breathe their work because it takes all of that and more to achieve what no one else has achieved before. The great inventors of the last century—Gates, Edison, Jobs, Einstein—completely immerse themselves in their quests to change the world and everything else in their lives must be put to the side. These rare people feel like they have been given a gift that must not be wasted. They are driven mostly by the mental challenge and the desire to make history and less by the need to make money or be socially powerful. Bill Gates is a good example of this. He will end up giving away most of the money he made and may be known as much for what his foundation has done to better the world as for what he did to change technology.

These great leaders and inventors mentioned above were able to achieve what they did because of their ability to be true to themselves. Their intense determination, dedication to achieving their goals, focus on the future, self-motivation, and interest in helping others led to success. These are all traits that are appreciated by everyone no matter what the environment. The ironic thing is that if you focus on who you are as a person, everything else tends to fall in place. Focus on being a certain "person" as opposed to a certain "thing."

CHAPTER 45

FOCUS ON THOSE THINGS THAT ACTUALLY MOVE THE NEEDLE

One thing that I have learned in my time in the financial industry and also through the founding of my business is the importance of time management. Many people are busy. However, the really successful ones are busy doing all the things necessary to move ahead. How you manage your time is a huge factor in how far you go in life. Successful people are much more efficient with their time as they seem to be better at eliminating busywork and frivolous activities. They do this by understanding what will get them paid, move them forward, or enrich personal relationships and by focusing as much time on those things as possible. They are not easily distracted. Today, many people appear to have Attention Deficit Disorder. They can't focus on one thing for too long and usually get pulled in several different directions and, as a result, nothing gets done to fruition.

When I was in sales, we used to be given very specific annual goals that we would be ranked on. These rankings would be a major factor in our compensation. I learned quickly that it was in my best interest to weed out all aspects of my job that kept me busy but were not in direct correlation to achieving these goals. There were certain salespeople who were always busy, but they would get sidetracked and start getting involved with things that took them off track. In order to move ahead, one has to learn to play the game. Don't try to argue what your goals are or should be. Just eliminate the wasted energy and do the things that will make you look good in the eyes of your bosses. Same thing with starting a business. You only have so much time in a day and a limited window to get your business off the ground. It becomes imperative to learn to prioritize and only focus on the things that will potentially lead to new clients or properly service your current ones.

Sometimes you have to decide whether the time you would spend on a project is worth the potential upside. Is this prospective new client just making me run around in circles? Are there bigger potential pieces of business that I should be focusing on? These are the critical decisions that determine the fates of businesses. The companies that succeed make the correct choices, the others don't. Sometimes even small decisions can cost your business time and money it can't afford. It is easy to fool yourself and spend your time doing a bunch of busywork because it is easier than the heavy lifting of sales work. Calling people and setting up business meetings is hard to do. You can fool yourself into thinking you are doing well because your schedule is full when, in reality, nothing is being done to move the needle. You get in early to work and leave late and run around to a lot of meetings. But are you actually creating results? Oftentimes executives at large corporations are enamored of all the wrong things. They fall in love with the employee that is the first one in the office or the one that is always running to meetings or walking really fast around the office never having time to sit down. Management holds them up as great examples, but many times these people don't have the goods to back up their outward appearances. It can often turn out to be an illusion.

It is the same with academics. Successful students learn to focus on the items in their studies that will get them good grades. They have a sense for what is important and what is not. They figure out what they need to work on, where their weaknesses are, and focus on these things instead of on the things that already come easy. Nobody wants to do the things that are difficult except the people that are successful. I have learned that really successful people do things with very little wasted effort. They do all the same things we do, but they get more done and also do the little things that others don't want to do.

Over time, it only takes a small change in your routine to improve your results. The student that studies just thirty minutes more a day ends up studying two and a half more hours a week, ten more hours a month and approximately eighty more hours in a given academic year. Who do you think will do better in school? The salesman that makes just four more sales calls a week ends up with sixteen more a month and two hundred more sales calls a year. Who do you think is going to have better numbers come bonus time? The person that goes to the gym three days a week instead of two ends up working out fifty more days annually. Who will be in better shape in the long term?

It takes minor adjustments in your life to make a huge difference in your success no matter what you are trying to accomplish. For one week try documenting how you spend your time. Actually log each hour you spend and how you are spending it and you will be amazed. At the end of the week you will find that much of your time is not going towards the things that are critical for you to achieve your goals, whatever they may be. You will learn to schedule your day better. Set aside time well in advance to do the things you need to do and don't get sidetracked by other things. Turn off your phone, turn off your computer, close the door and do whatever you need to do to focus. Don't let your mind trick you into thinking you are doing everything you need to do to get ahead when it may not be the case.

CHAPTER 46

COME TO TERMS WITH YOUR WEAKNESSES

Your strengths are what get you noticed. Everyone focuses on what they do very well as these are the things that bring results and recognition. It is fun to focus on these things because they come easily to you. However, over the long term, you will only go as far as your weaknesses will allow. The world is full of immensely talented people who didn't meet their potential or fell from grace because their weaknesses eventually led to their downfall. The executive that isn't honest, the musician with an alcohol addiction, the athlete with a drug issue, the executive with a communication problem, the manager with control issues.

But beyond the big issues, there are also minor shortcomings that keep us from reaching our potential every day. They may not bring us down, but they keep us from moving forward. Maybe you don't take care of your health, you don't do enough to look your best, you are never on time, or are afraid of talking in front of larger groups. There are many little things we could do to improve our marketability both in the workplace and out. If you are a pitcher and you can throw your fastball at ninety-five miles an hour, you will be a star in high school and college. But once you get to the big leagues where all the batters are exceptional, you will not succeed without a curveball. The fastball gets you noticed, the fastball brings success, the lack of a curveball brings you down. The student who gets mostly A's in school but never does well in math. The A's get her noticed; the one C keeps her from getting in to a top college.

Successful people come to terms with their weaknesses. They admit they need help in certain areas and seek out a solution. They can either address their flaws directly and do everything possible to improve on them, or they might choose to bring in others to assist with these areas. No one is good at everything, and smart leaders recognize this. They make sure they surround themselves with people who are experts in key areas and then they put their trust in them. Ego is the most dangerous weakness because it prevents you from recognizing your faults. People influenced by ego can't admit to any weaknesses. They downplay their faults and, in most cases, are blind to them. As a result, they never get addressed, which in turn eventually leads to a downfall. Tiger Woods had a weakness. He didn't address it, and it changed his life. Bill Clinton had a flaw, it almost brought him down, but certainly kept him from reaching his full potential. Understand that over the long run your weaknesses will always be exposed. Stress reveals your weakest point. This is why the military is so strict about who they admit because, as they always say, the enemy will always expose your weakest flank. The opponent will always expose your weakest player. Be clear, we all have flaws. The best way to determine them is to simply be confident enough to ask the people around you to help you identify them and then come to terms with them. Once you have done this, work equally as hard on your weaknesses as your strengths and do your best to put yourself in situations where the latter are highlighted and the former minimized.

CHAPTER 47

DON'T BELIEVE EVERYTHING YOU READ OR HEAR

O ne of the things that my liberal arts education taught me was to intellectually challenge many of the assertions that are presented. I learned not to take everything at face value. Though I find that most people are guilty of this. If it is in writing, on television news, or communicated by a friend, they believe it. They often do not challenge or verify what they deem to be facts. For many people, this information does not go through any filtering process in their brain. It goes in their ears and out their mouth.

However, it is important to understand that everyone has an agenda and a natural bias of some kind. Some worse than others, most are unconscious, but everyone has them. This results in all information being affected in some way as it is released. Of course, there are very extreme examples of this. Even the heralded *New York Times* has run into issues, having to admit that certain stories were not completely accurate. Dan Rather, the anchor of CBS News was let go from his job for running a story that was less than fully accurate. Brian Williams met the same fate except his lies were about himself. These are trusted names in news dissemination.

One of the most famous cases of inaccurate information was the high profile case of *Rolling Stone Magazine* running a story about a student being raped on the campus of UVA. A story that ended up having no basis in fact. The truth eventually revealed itself, but not before many people's lives had been deeply affected. The same thing happened to the Duke lacrosse team ten years ago. Several players were implicated in an allegation of rape. In a story that quickly went national, students' reputations were tarnished. It was a terrible story, but one that ended up not being true either. People in both cases jumped to conclusions and acted based on totally false information. Of course, these are very extreme examples and the problem can occur with even the most respected journalistic entities. The *New York Times*, for instance, had to admit years ago that one of its journalists had been let go due to instances of plagiarism and fabrication. I am not suggesting that everything you read or hear is not true. What I am suggesting is that most information is affected by some sort of filter that has the ability to alter it in some way. We all know that in a game of telephone, by the time the original message gets all the way around the circle it is completely different. Everyone's brain filters information differently.

Furthermore, everyone has an agenda. Most people are trying to sell you something or they have a vested interest in how you think about something. A large factor in the financial collapse was the fact that financial institutions wanted to sell certain mortgage-backed securities. They were making a lot of money for firms. They were selling securities they knew were not appropriate for some people. Publicly they had positive things to say about investments that they knew had large risk profiles. The result was that many people ended up owning securities that became worthless. These firms later received large penalties for how they had gone about selling these securities. The medical industry went through similar changes because the government found that doctors were receiving benefits for the prescribing of certain medicines. Certainly this is not the way medicine should be allocated. Finally, just take a look at the election of 2016 between Trump and Clinton. Television news teams, newspapers, and pollsters did not have their finest moment. Very few of these institutions got it right. Most every poll had Clinton winning. News people were saying it could be a landslide and over by 8 pm in favor of Clinton and even the *New York Times* afterwards came out and said that they could have done a better job on their coverage of the election. Sometimes people project news based on the way they see the world as opposed to hard facts. Make sure you use your own filter.

We have all heard gossip about people we know, some of which can be very harmful. Looking back, how many times has this hearsay been 100% accurate? Not often. There may be a kernel of truth to them, but often these rumors are highly exaggerated. The information you receive can be slightly altered with context or mitigating facts omitted. In either case it may affect how you view that information. For instance, I recently watched a documentary on the infamous JonBenét Ramsey case—the unsolved death of an eight-year-old child that garnered immense media coverage for many years. This documentary reviewed all of the evidence and had a panel of different experts providing their opinion and insight. Upon completion of the show you were left with a very clear opinion of what they thought happened, and I agreed at the time. However, several hours later on the exact same network was another show that focused on the case and included interviews with members of the family. Upon reviewing the case, this show left you with a very different feeling of what had happened. So I was right back where I began, not having any idea about what really happened. Neither of these shows was lying or making up facts. But they both decided to stress particular pieces of evidence and focus on the testimony of certain witnesses as opposed to others. Each show took a certain point of view and the way in which each presented what they call "the facts" resulted in a completely different conclusion. The same can be said for the Kennedy assassination. Each documentary you watch about that event will leave you with a different feeling of what happened as well.

So the next time you receive a noteworthy piece of information, before you react to it or pass it on, analyze it. Sometimes it makes sense to sit on it for a while to let the facts shake out. But don't be afraid to use what you know and your insight to analyze the veracity of the information before you react to it. Ask yourself, who is giving me this information? What is their relation to the situation? What do they have invested in the outcome? Have the facts been vetted? Don't react quickly to information that doesn't make sense to you, for sometimes there is good reason it doesn't add up.

CHAPTER 48

WHEN IN DOUBT, TAKE MONEY OUT OF THE EQUATION

There are times in life when we can't seem to make a decision. We go back and forth on what to do. As discussed in a previous chapter, the best thing to do in these situations is to trust your gut. But another way to handle these situations is to figure out what you would do if you took money out of the equation. Almost all big decisions involve a financial component. Obviously, there are fringe situations where an option isn't remotely financially possible and others where money is no object. However, these usually don't pose as difficult decisions. What I am suggesting, in general, is that you don't avoid doing something you feel is important because of money. Conversely, don't do something just because of the money. These usually turn out to be decisions you regret. There are times when financial decisions align completely with your skills, goals, values, or lifestyle. There are also times when nothing aligns. In these cases, it helps to ask yourself what you would do if money wasn't a factor.

One of the key areas where this can become an issue is the choice of a spouse. Unfortunately, money can at times come into play in these decisions. People choosing to marry someone because they have a lot of money or, conversely, not moving forward long-term with them because of a lack of it. Of course, some people do not have the ability to assess themselves honestly in these situations. They tell themselves that money is not a factor, but the inner self may have a different take on that. Money is the number one cause of divorce. It is a stress on a marriage if you don't have enough and, believe it or not, it can take relationships to difficult places if you have too much. I have seen people break up with people they liked very much because they didn't like the lifestyle they envisioned living with that person only to regret the breakup years later. People can and do change a lot over time, so as long as you see the correct character and drive in these people, what they do for a living when in their twenties should be irrelevant. I have also seen people marry for money. They were marrying the lifestyle and not the person. I don't have to tell you that your lifestyle can change quickly and is irrelevant when stress hits the relationship, as it inevitably does, no matter how much money you have.

Money can also affect your decision to take advantage of a lifetime opportunity. Usually, the benefits that come from partaking in these opportunities far outweigh the costs in the long term. Is there a trip you or your family could go on to do something memorable or visit a relative? Is there a class you can take to further your education? Are there things you can do to further your career? These investments of money and time usually pay big dividends.

My stepfather fought in WWII stationed in one of the most brutal areas of the German front—The Hurtgen Forest. Veterans rarely talk about their time in battle. So, when as an eighty-year-old, he decided to take his family back to retrace his steps in the war, it was a trip that I had to find a way to do. The trip turned out to have a huge impact on all of us and helped us understand the man in a way we couldn't have otherwise. Similarly, several years ago I took an overnight trip with my son that also impacted our relationship. My alma mater, Yale University, is certainly not known for its sports programs. So, when the school's hockey team had a chance to play in the NCAA National Championship game I could not let the opportunity go by. The school had never won a national championship in any major sport, and I certainly wasn't going to miss the chance to see the first one happen. Yale was a very large underdog in the game, having already lost to their opponent three times that season. But I told my son we had to be there just in case. We jumped in the car, found some tickets and a hotel, and drove five hours to Pittsburgh for the game. Yale ended up pulling off a huge upset and won the game. My son and I were there to see it, and we have been talking about it ever since. It was a bonding experience that could not be replicated. The investment in time and money created a memory that we will never forget and strengthened what was already a strong relationship.

You have heard the old adage, "you have to spend money to make money." As a business owner you have to make crucial decisions all the time about what to invest in that will take your company to the next level. You can't grow without investing in yourself and your career or business. The risk comes in making the right investment decisions, because rarely can you invest in everything. Those that don't invest stay static and get left behind. The same can be said for your personal life. You will have to make investments of time and money in order to move forward as a person and in your relationships. So, when faced with a decision, if you would definitely do it if money were not a factor, then it often makes sense to move forward in the long run. In the end, life is about your memories and relationships.

CHAPTER 49

DON'T FORGET THOSE THAT HAVE LAID THE GROUNDWORK FOR YOU

It doesn't matter who you are, what you do, or where you come from, someone has laid the groundwork for you to be you. Of course, you need to be yourself and become your own person to be successful, but no one got to be where they are without certain people having set the stage for them. First, let's start with your parents. No matter what your relationship with them, you have to admit that they provided the framework, in some form or fashion, for you to have a head on your shoulders. It is important to recognize this fact and give back to these people as you reach your peak and they move well past theirs. While we all are responsible for our own success, it is impossible to get there by going out on a limb by yourself. If not your parents, then someone held that role for you, whether it be a mentor, relative, teacher, or coach. We are all shaped by these important people along the way, and often their influence is very subtle. The way your coach approached each game, the positive reinforcement supplied by a teacher, or just the environment provided by a relative that allowed you to flourish. All successful people have some sort of strong foundation from which to build. You developed your character from someone, so come to terms with this and pay homage to them, otherwise ego is sure to bloom.

On a far larger scale, if you live in the United States, you have so many people to thank for your existence as you know it today. The greatness of this country has been shaped by so many people before us, and unfortunately many of us take that for granted. History is humbling. On my desk are two things that remind me that today could look a lot different if it weren't for those that have come before us.

First, I have a miniature version of the Constitution of the United States. The fact that our forefathers united to create a document well over two hundred years ago that would serve as the foundation for the greatest country in the world should be lost on no one. Its brilliance lies in the fact that it was so well thought out that it is still relevant and serving as the backbone of our modern society today. It is a timeless document. Americans owe much of what they take for granted every day to this document. I shudder to think where we would be today without it.

The second thing on my desk is a picture I took of the cemetery at Normandy Beach. It is a picture of hundreds and hundreds of simple white crosses that mark the burial ground of those who lost their lives there defending our freedom. All Americans should be required to visit Normandy during their lifetime, preferably as early as possible. Any student of history can only be humbled by the large cliffs that sit before you while you stand there on the beach and envision what it looked like more than seventy years ago with the bodies of so many Americans strewn across it.

The reason the picture resonates so much with me is that if you focus on the very front of the picture, you see the name on one cross. You can focus on that one life and reflect on it. However, if your eyes move to the back of the photo, the crosses become just one big white blur. It becomes impossible to discern any individual names or even where one cross ends and the other begins. As a matter of fact, if you just looked at the back of the photo, it would be impossible to determine what it is depicting at all. That is how many crosses there are and how close the burial spots are to each other. The sheer number of people buried there becomes hard to digest and understand. It becomes easy to just glance over the magnitude of the sacrifice that was made and hard to individualize it.

Both of these items on my desk help ground me and allow me to remember that many people came before me and laid the groundwork that allows me to live the life I live today. There are people that lived a hundred years ago that should be thanked for this, and there are those people in your lives today that also should be recognized. Some Americans go about their lives with no appreciation of this. They feel entitled to live a certain life and get upset when a certain lifestyle is not handed to them on a silver platter. In order to appreciate what you have and to live a grounded and fulfilled life, do what you need to do to recognize those that have come before you.

CHAPTER 50

IN THE END IT'S
ALL UP TO YOU

Throughout this book, I have provided insight that I have gathered throughout the fifty years of my existence that I believe would be helpful to guide one through life. Many of these involve how to treat, trust, and communicate with people. No one can get anywhere completely on his or her own. Actually, you can, but it is a lot more difficult path to take. But the last word of wisdom that I can provide may perhaps be the most important and doesn't involve other people. It involves you and only you.

My last piece of advice is for you to quickly understand that, in the end, your success, happiness, and ability to live a fulfilled life starts and ends with you. The buck stops here. You have to look out for yourself first because, in the end, no one else is looking out for you. You can't look for handouts, either. No one is responsible for your behavior and position in life other than you. There are people that look out for you sometimes and, if you are lucky, more often than that. However, no one is looking out for you all the time. You have to always make sure that your interests and those of your loved ones are protected. This is particularly true in times of stress and difficulty because it is in these times that people around you act irrationally, selfishly, and sometimes immorally. These negative traits do not show themselves during normal times, but rather in difficult ones.

I am not, in any way, suggesting that you shouldn't trust people or incorporate others into all aspects of your lives. As a matter of fact, the only way you will ever get ahead in life is to surround yourself with good people and allow other people to help you. All great leaders have to eventually delegate responsibilities in order to move the larger group ahead, including themselves. However, it is important to make sure you know these people well, how they operate, and their strengths and weaknesses. Even then you need to make sure your interests are always covered as well. You need to make sure that you develop above average skills in the workplace that are useful and in demand by others in order to survive. This way you become much more invaluable to the organization. It is up to you to determine and develop these skills.

When I was working in the financial services industry for a major Fortune 500 company, there were several times when the company and industry went through tumultuous periods. There were senior management changes, and everyone's job status was up in the air. During one of these times, I went to visit a friend of mine in senior management. Someone that I could talk to about my career and who would provide guidance. I will never forget one of these conversations during which I asked him about my status and about making it through these tough periods and layoffs. He responded by saying, "Stuart, I got enough problems on my end to even begin to think about your situation. I am trying to make it through myself." This conversation taught me that when the chips are down, we all have to look out for ourselves and may not necessarily have time to worry about others. It never occurred to me that he would have to worry about the same things as I. It makes perfect sense, but it is easy to be myopic and assume that others are focused on you when they aren't. In the end, this senior person was eventually moved out of his job at the firm.

The other memory I have that always brings this message home for me is the time that I took two Navy Seals to lunch. This was as a part of my event management company, and I was introduced to them with the idea that I might be able to help them get speaking appearances. When we sat down at the table along with a few other people, the Navy Seals told me that they were trained to always sit with their backs to the wall in the corner of the room. From this vantage point they could keep an eye on everyone that came into the room and see if anything unusual happened so that they could react quickly. While there was absolutely zero reason to worry at this venue as we were eating at a private club with mostly successful executives in the room, they were still keeping an eye out on the entire room. This taught me that it makes sense on some level to always keep an eye out for worst-case scenarios and be in a position to react to them.

In the end, if you want something to happen, you have to make it happen yourself. No one else is going to hand it to you. Don't rely on others to come through for you. If they do, that is gravy, but don't go through life relying on others to pave the way for you. You control your own destiny.

BONUS CHAPTER

I like to tell stories. Unfortunately for my audience, I tend to painfully drag these stories out. Therefore, it was to my great surprise that when I got to the end of writing this book I realized that somehow I had not included one of my favorite stories that virtually all my friends have heard ad infinitum. I didn't feel that in good conscience I could submit this book to publication without including it. Since we learned in Chapter 41 that it is unwise to try and force a square peg into a round hole, I decided that instead of injecting the story into one of the completed chapters, this story warranted a chapter all its own. Therefore, I present to you the following bonus chapter.

CHAPTER 51

THE PERILS OF "SPELLCHECK"

A s a junior at Yale, I had to write a "junior" thesis as part of the requirements for my major. This assignment actually took place during the first semester of my senior year and was "junior" in the sense that it prepared you for the writing of the all-important senior thesis later that year. Even so, it is a serious and significant assignment that takes months to complete.

As I started the project, I realized that it might make sense to ask my dad if I could borrow his desktop computer to work on the project. It was a Compaq computer which, at the time, along with IBM, was the leader in individual computers. Given that the year was 1985, computers in dorm rooms were uncommon to say the least. As a matter of fact, looking back I can't think of one friend that owned any sort of computer. The ability to use it was a complete luxury.

I came to the end of my paper. It was somewhere between twenty and thirty pages long. The night before it was due, I was in my dorm giving the final product one last proofread when a classmate and friend walked into my room. As I stared with intense focus at the computer screen, scrolling through the pages, he asked me what I was doing. I explained that I was proofreading the paper one last time. He seemed perplexed as to why I was doing it manually and asked if I had ever heard of something called "spellcheck." I responded that I had not. He told me that he had interned over the summer at IBM and knew about this computer feature that allowed the computer, with a click of a button, to scroll through the document and check for misspellings and other issues. I told him that I was done with the paper and, at this point, I wasn't sure this step was necessary. After more coaxing and assurances, I moved out of my chair and let him show me how it worked. A seemingly harmless decision that soon came back to haunt me.

My friend sat down, took control of the mouse, and clicked on a button. After a few seconds, the computer started making a funny noise, and the screen started flashing in and out. Since I was new to the computer world, I calmly asked him if this was normal. He did not seem concerned and said to give it a minute as he was familiar with the IBM version of this feature. However, after another minute of this, my anxiety level grew as I could see a slight look of discomfort come over my friend's face as he fidgeted in the chair. I started pacing back and forth as he started helplessly pressing certain keys on the keyboard harder and harder, each time hoping for a different result.

At this point, he asked me if I had saved the document to a disk, which I had. He kept saying, "We should be fine, you saved it didn't you?" The computer screen just kept surging in and out like it was eating the words for dinner and, at this point, my friend just stopped banging keys and left the room. I was left alone with the monster of a computer just staring me in the face with a blank screen. There was no sign of my paper anywhere.

My shock soon turned to anger, which would only increase after what happened next. I got on the phone and called my professor. Keep in mind, this was late in the evening and well before cell phones existed. Somehow, I reached him. I explained what had happened to which he responded that he had heard too many other people try to blame an unfinished paper on a computer malfunction and that, if the paper was not on his desk in the morning, I would fail the assignment.

I proceeded to take out my frustration on anything in my room that was not nailed down. At this point, my friends and hall mates, gathered outside, and word was beginning to spread about what had happened. My friends blocked the hallway so others were not innocently caught up in the dismantling of my room. At this point, a good friend took it upon himself to go to bat for me. He walked over to the dorm's dean and explained the situation. He told him all the facts and assured him that the paper had actually been completed and that it was not some sort of excuse. The dean picked up the phone and called the professor. The dean suggested that he would call the Yale Computer Science Department to see if their experts would take a look at the disk and try to retrieve the paper. The professor agreed.

The next day, I took the disk over to the computer science department. Out came three men who didn't look like they saw the light of day very much. They took my disk and very confidently told me they would be back soon with a printout of my paper. I took a seat in the waiting room, feeling better about things. I sat and sat some more with no sign of any computer scientists. Eventually, one man came out and handed me one sheet of paper. It had about three sentences on it and some random groups of words.

"This is all we could come up with," he said as he quickly retreated back into his world. A document of over twenty pages had been reduced to a few sentences.

I walked back to the dorm in a state of despair and handed the piece of paper to my dean who called my professor. After a discussion with the dean, he agreed to let me rewrite the paper over Christmas vacation. I had to spend my whole break rewriting a paper that had been completely finished. Needless to say, I wrote it in pencil on a yellow legal pad. It turned out later that Compaq had some sort of "bug" with their spellcheck application. I was so very glad I could serve as a guinea pig for the novel home computer industry (please pick up on the high degree of sarcasm here).

Now, over dinner and a few cocktails, I can drag this story out for at least a half an hour, if desired. There are friends of mine that know this all too well. This story could have served as an example in many chapters of this book. It plays into the idea that nothing is done until it is done, and even then it is not done. It serves as an example of the fact that you just never know who is going to go out of their way to help you when the chips are down. Finally, timing certainly played a role in this story as well. But most of all, it is just a funny story. It has been over 30 years and I can now finally laugh about it.

ACKNOWLEDGEMENTS

I would like to thank the following women for their help with the production of this book: Faith, Meg, and Ann. Faith for her editing skills, Meg for her designing skills, and Ann for allowing me to cash in some of my "Platinum" points.

This is Stuart's first and, quite possibly, only book. As of its writing, he has lived quite an average life. He has never run a Fortune 500 company, been elected to office, served as quarterback for a Super Bowl-winning team, nor has he ever pioneered a new product development that changed the way the world works. Therefore, you are under no obligation to heed the advice put forth on these pages.

Stuart started his career in the sports and sports marketing industry. He also worked for over a decade in the financial services industry. He founded and now runs an event management company that focuses on unique, high-end corporate events. He earned a B.A. from Yale University. He has an awesome wife and two terrific kids.